MW01716387

BEACH BUM

A Life in Pieces

BEACH BUM

A Life in Pieces

ROBERT "Butch" FREEDMAN

INKWATER PRESS
PORTLAND • OREGON
INKWATERPRESS.COM

Cover and interior design by Masha Shubin

Cover background: Tropical Beack Background © Val_Iva. BigStockPhoto.com

Publisher: Inkwater Press | www.inkwaterpress.com

ISBN-13 978-1-62901-568-2 | ISBN-10 1-62901-568-7

1 3 5 7 9 10 8 6 4 2

For Jessica and Gabrielle

“The cure for anything is salt water: sweat, tears, or the sea.”

Isak Dinesen

“Be patient. Wave come. Wave always come.”

Duke Kahanamoku

Table of Contents

Part Three
RUNNING WITH BLINDERS

Part Four
TRYING TO FIND HOME

Part Five
GETTING ON, GETTING OLD

An Introduction of Sorts

Like many of my generation I've spent much time and energy trying to "find myself." I've looked everywhere – in different parts of the country, different religions and philosophies, different jobs, different women, different drugs. I probably shouldn't have bothered (though I won't discredit the trip), since what I was looking for was never very far away. I knew it when I was a kid, forgot about it in middle age, and know it again as an old man. I am a beach bum.

When I was a boy it was the Jersey Shore where I thrived. The summers at the Shore were what I looked forward to all year in cold and grey Philadelphia. It was only when my dad drove the family to Long Beach Island and announced that he had bought a small cottage there that I knew in the depths of my being where I belonged. All summer long I went barefoot, swam every day in the ocean, collected shells and beach glass, learned how to crab and fish and to body surf. Though I wouldn't have had the words for it then, it was at the edge of the continent, and only there that I felt fully alive, fully in the world.

When I was 18 I went away to college in the Midwest and the long drought followed. You know, life gets in the way. Marriage, family, jobs, and oh yeah, that aforementioned searching. Somehow I allowed my love of the ocean and its powerful draw to slip away. Sure, there were the occasional visits that reminded me of how much I loved the beach, but I was of a mind then that ignored the obvious signals, and instead listened to the ancient whispers that I needed to be responsible, serious, live up to expectations – whose I was never quite sure. I gave up too much in exchange for too little. But I never did entirely forget about the ocean. Knew always the siren call.

In my forties, after we had moved from Seattle to Oregon, I convinced my then-wife that we should buy a house at the Oregon Coast, even though we had little money and didn't own a home in the inland town where I was teaching high school classes. Surprisingly she agreed, and we made a small down payment on a house in Gearhart, Oregon, a lovely little beach town on the North Coast. We went there almost every weekend and vacation, and I remembered once again what it was like to be happy. My daughters learned to love the beach as much as I did. The girls would pick wildflowers from the dunes to decorate our dinner table. I lobbied to move us to the Coast full-time. "I can get a job maybe at Seaside High School," I told them. But the call of the city and friends was too strong. My family wanted things to stay as they were. I understood.

More years passed and my oldest was off to college, and Cathy and I came to a place where we knew things had to change. We divorced. And later I sold the house in Gearhart and moved back to Seattle. Both my daughters warned me that I would regret that sale. Gabrielle even cried when I told her. Of course, they were right. I don't know what I was thinking.

Twenty more years passed and I got lucky. Met a woman who is now my wife and who loves the beach as much as me. Bev and I bought a home in Cape Meares, Oregon. If you don't know where that is, good. We like to keep it quiet. Now, every day, I get to be a kid again, walking on the beach, collecting agates, listening to the pounding waves, day dreaming, and once again surfing. Every morning I look out from our upstairs deck to check if the surf will allow me to get out there. When it does, I pull on my wetsuit and go. There's no more searching to be done. I'm right where and who I want to be. I am a beach bum once again. These stories will recount at least a part of that journey.

Part One

Kid Stuff

Call Me Butch

If you phoned up my family home in Philadelphia and asked to speak to Robert, the person who answered would tell you that you had the wrong number. And if you shook me awake in the middle of the night screaming, "Rob, get out! There's a fire," I'd think, "Who the hell is Rob?" Nonetheless, most of the people I will speak with or do business with today will know me only as Rob. You see, I'm a guy who's lost his name. And I'm not at all happy about it.

So what is your true name, you may ask. And a fine question it is, which allows me to tell the following story, as related to me on a fairly regular basis throughout my childhood by my mother and her two sisters, Aunt Elaine and Aunt Genevieve (my grandfather had a thing for Tennyson). The story was not told to me by my father because he was not around at the time I was named, being otherwise engaged in Army Air Corp service overseas. Here's what happened.

There was a trolley strike in Philadelphia that hot August night in 1944 when my mother went into labor and since my father was, as I mentioned, elsewhere and my aunts didn't drive, there was no way to get to the hospital. After a few frantic hours, a cab was located and the three sisters arrived at Mt. Sinai Hospital with only moments to spare before I plopped on out – a ruddy, screaming baby boy who the receiving nurse could barely handle. "My god, he's a big one," she said. My mother, probably still in shock and exhausted, gladly let the attending nurses whisk me away to be cleaned and weighed and whatever else is done to newborns. When they brought me back, the nurses were laughing. "What's the big joke?" my mother asked, in no mood for frivolity.

"He weighs eleven and a half pounds," the nurse said. "A new record here." I imagine my mother groaned and held out her arms anyway, resigned to her heavy burden. "The other girls are calling him Butch," the nurse told Mom. "You know, because he's so chubby and all."

"I've named him Robert," my mother, a formidable woman, stated. "He is not a Butch." But Aunt Gen and Aunt Elaine were standing right there and they must have thought Butch had a certain cachet because by the time Mom and I left Mt. Sinai a few days later, Robert had disappeared. My name was Butch.

And it stayed Butch throughout all my school years, on into college and beyond. Sure, every once in a while a teacher would slip and call me Robert as was noted on her student roster, but the laughter of the rest of the students would quickly bring her to scratch out the given name and write in my now permanent nickname.

I should mention here that I didn't continue on in life as a big and burly sort of guy. And I wasn't tough or mean or a schoolyard bully – well, there was that one incident with Gary Erlbaum, but that was hardly worthy of a Butch or a Spike or even an Archie. Despite any connotations, I liked the name. It was mine. Butch was who I was. You don't question things like that.

It was when I started teaching that things went south. Of course, students called me Mr. Freedman, so that wasn't a problem. But my fellow faculty members? Well, somehow I decided that they had expectations of me – the new young teacher – that I had to live up to. How appropriate would it be to hold out my hand and introduce myself as Butch Freedman?

"Butch?" I thought they'd say, recoiling in horror. "A teacher can hardly be a Butch. Are you mad?"

So I caved in and told everyone my name was Rob. Robert was too stuffy, I reasoned. And I would never want to be a Bob or Bobby. Rob struck just the right note – friendly, but still professional. My colleagues seemed to accept it. The name stuck. Dammit all to hell. I became a Rob.

A number of times over the years, I've tried to reclaim my name. But it never seemed to take. Once you've crossed over into the straight name world, it's hard to turn back. Sure my family still calls me Butch, and old school friends do also – and the occasional intimate acquaintance would, when I asked, use it in the bedroom. I liked that. Still I wanted more. I wanted to be myself.

So, I'm trying again now. I'm too old to be bothered by other people's expectations, and not at all concerned about being judged. Come to think of it, did anyone other than myself, ever actually judge me about my name? I now seriously doubt it. Still, it's been rough going. Even my sweet wife, who first met me as a Rob, finds it hard to remember to call me Butch. Though when she does, I think we both feel closer. Other friends and acquaintances are harder. If I want them to address me correctly, I would have to keep reminding them to do so, and I don't have the heart or patience for that. So I let it go and don't take offense. I'm getting much better at that whole thing too, the not-getting-upset-when-you-don't-get-what-you-want thing. Most of the time, I'm grateful just to be getting out of bed in the morning.

Not too long ago, I returned to Philadelphia for my 50th high school reunion. I had a much better time than I thought I would and mostly recognized all my aged classmates. To me, they looked not all that different than they did when we walked down the aisle at graduation. We had a great time reminiscing and catching up – and dancing to Chubby Checker and Danny and The Juniors, but, best of all, every single one of those fine old friends called me Butch – as if I'd never had any other name.

Dinner at the Chinese Restaurant

I loved going to the Chinese Restaurant. It likely had a more specific name, but it's not one I ever remember any of us using. We all simply called it the Chinese Restaurant. And when my dad announced that we were going there for dinner, my brother and I could not contain our excitement and began leaping up and down.

We would all pile into the family car – a grayish 1954 Buick sedan – Mom and Dad in the front seat, the three of us in the back. My older sister Linda sat strategically between me and Paul, so we wouldn't fool around and make Dad angry enough to stop the car and say, "One more word and we're going to turn around and go home. Is that what you want?"

And we'd both look down and say, no that wasn't what we wanted at all we really, truly, deeply wanted to go to the Chinese Restaurant and we would be good boys from now on we promised, swear to God. Linda looked smug, glad we were getting what we deserved. She was convinced we were the most annoying brothers in the world. She may have even been willing to give up the Chinese dinner just to see us punished. But, in the end, we all knew, including Dad, that he was not going to turn around and take us home. Not now, not when we were so close to Chinatown we could almost smell the fishy odors wafting through the open car windows, just like when we were getting near the ocean at the Jersey Shore and could smell the salt air.

Dad turned back to the front, put the car in gear, and drove on, and my brother and I looked at each other, over Linda, and grinned.

Chinatown in Philadelphia was down by the waterfront in the few blocks surrounding the approach to the Ben Franklin Bridge. I always thought it was strange that a neighborhood could be named in such a way. It would be like someone calling our West Philadelphia neighborhood Jew Town or parts of North Philly, Negro Place. But the people in Chinatown didn't seem to mind, as far as I could tell. All the shops and restaurants announced it on their storefronts. Maybe they were proud of being Chinese and didn't want to be mixed up with the rest of us. Their food was sure different and a whole lot better, I thought, than the stuff we ate back in Jew Town.

The hostess always seemed unusually happy to see us, smiling and bowing and quickly leading us to our favorite table, right near the fish tank – a beautiful, big, bubbling aquarium with all sorts of colorful tropical fish swimming around. My brother and I were big fans of tropical fish. We had our own cloudy ten gallon aquarium at home where we raised guppies and black mollys, and tiny little catfish; but our aquarium was dwarfed by the one here at the Chinese Restaurant, which was crystal clear and had to be at least 100 gallons and full of odd looking fish, some of which seemed big enough to eat. Paul and I argued later about the fate of those fish.

We didn't even have to read the menus. We all knew what we wanted. But we looked anyway, just to be polite. Being polite was important. I don't remember talking very much before we ordered. Our family wasn't very chatty. I don't think Dad felt he had anything to say to children and we kids knew we weren't supposed to bother him. Mom always warned us about this: "Don't talk to your father," she'd say. "He's got too much on his mind." I always wondered what terrible things were going on in his head, but I knew better than to ask. I had learned the hard way not to irritate my father.

But at the Chinese restaurant the mood was more easy going. Sometimes Dad would even smile and tell Mom some story about one of his patients. And he wouldn't even get mad if Paul and I started laughing about something or began teasing Linda.

When the Chinese waitress came to take our order, Dad was, of course, the one who spoke. "We'll start with the egg rolls," he told her, speaking slowly in his deep doctor's voice. My taste buds were already throbbing, thinking about the golden brown, crispy rolls that would soon arrive along with the fiery hot mustard that you could dip your section of egg roll into if you dared. "And we'll have Won Ton soup," Dad told her. It was only years later that I discovered there were other types of Chinese soups.

"Then we'll have a double order of spare ribs." Paul and I could hardly sit still at this point. Spare ribs were our absolute favorites. More bone than meat, but so tasty and greasy. What could be better than eating food with your hands, and right in front of your father without him reaching over and smacking your hand with his fork. "Also we'll have the Chow Mein." He waited for the waitress to write it down on her pad, but she was nodding and smiling, way ahead of him.

Then sometimes Dad would look at me and nod, which meant I got to tell the waitress the next dish. "Moo Goo Gai Pan," I almost shouted. Dad must have known how much I loved to say that name. I didn't care so much about the dish itself, something full of chicken and mushrooms and other vegetables, but the name was magical. Moo Goo Gai Pan.

Then it was Mom's turn to order, and like everything else, it was always the same. "And I will have the shrimp in oyster sauce." It somehow seemed so elegant and exotic – two foods that we never ate at home and here combined into one dish.

We didn't have to order the bowls of white rice or the hot tea; we knew the waitress would bring those without asking. That's how wonderful eating at the Chinese restaurant was. Hot tea in little porcelain cups and all our favorite dishes served under gleaming metal covers, and all of us passing the platters and the rice around the table and Dad asking who was ready for more soup to be ladled into their bowl and Mom smiling as she forked up her pink shrimp, and for at least that moment I could believe we were a happy family.

By the time the fortune cookies were delivered along with the check, Paul and I felt brave enough to read the silly messages out loud: “You will meet a dark stranger.” “Healthy life can be yours.” “One’s love is like the ocean.” “Keep always a happy face.” Even Mom and Linda joined in. We all were laughing. I wanted it to go on and on. I wanted us to live forever in the Chinese Restaurant.

But after Dad had paid the check and left a few extra dollars on the table for a tip, he cinched up his loosened tie, slipped back into his jacket, and said, “Okay, we’re all done here. It’s time to go back.”

“No, please,” I burst out. “I don’t wanta leave.” Mom shot a warning look in my direction. But Dad just stared straight ahead, as if I wasn’t even there.

Best Friends

He was a skinny kid who wore thick horn-rimmed glasses. I was a skinny kid too, and George and I were best friends. We lived in the same neighborhood, walked home from junior high together, and we both liked collecting baseball cards. That's all we needed to be best friends.

George and I decided we wanted to have leather motorcycle hats, the kind that Marlon Brando wore in "The Wild Ones." We saved our allowance money for months, then walked down to the Penn campus to a store that sold them. It was very exciting. I bought the traditional black hat, but George decided to buy a red leather one. When we walked out of the store with our hats proudly on our heads, a flock of pigeons flew overhead, and each and every one of those damn birds dropped a glob of gooey white birdshit right on top of George's new red hat. Not one of them shit on me.

George was an awful mess, white goo all over his

new hat and running on to his face. I started to laugh, until I saw that George was crying. I tried then to help him clean up, but there wasn't much I could do. On the way home, I told George he could have my hat. He thought about it, then said that, no, he didn't want it. And "Who needs a damn motorcycle hat anyway?" I didn't say anything else, because I could tell George didn't really want to talk about it.

When I got back to my house I wanted to show off the new hat to my brother and sister – and to my parents also, so I kept it on my head and swaggered on into our living room. It was right before dinner, so Linda, my sister, and Paulie, my younger brother were watching TV and Dad was trying to read his newspaper. They looked up when I came in, but then turned back to what they were doing. I was disappointed – of course.

"Hey," I said, "What's everybody doing?"

Nobody answered, cause I guess the answer was obvious. They were doing what they were doing. After another minute, Dad dropped the paper into his lap and stared at me. "What the hell is that?" he said.

I was taken aback by his tone, but still pleased in some odd way that he was finally noticing me. "It's a motorcycle hat," I said, and took the hat off my head to point to the emblem of a wheel with wings above the bill.

"Why do you need a motorcycle hat?" Dad asked.

"Well, I don't need it," I said, still not understanding why he sounded angry, "I just wanted it." I took a breath, but when no one said anything, I stumbled on. "George got one too. A red one. But then the pigeons pooped on it and he had to throw it away."

Paulie started laughing. Dad went back to his newspaper.

"It's not funny," I yelled. "We saved up a long time."

"You and your friend are ridiculous," Linda piped up. She was older than me by three years and always acted like she knew everything. "That hat looks dumb on you."

"How come the pigeons didn't get you?" Paulie asked. I could tell he wasn't being mean like Linda. He just wanted to know.

"Maybe they were aiming at the red," I said. "It's easier to see."

"Maybe," Paul said.

"You really are an idiot," Linda said. "You think pigeons make group decisions?"

"Shut up, pimple-face," I yelled at her.

"That's enough," Dad commanded. "Be quiet. All of you."

"I thought you'd like it," I said. I wasn't even sure who I was talking to. I heard Linda snicker.

"Just go get ready for dinner now," Dad said to me, pointing me up the stairs to the bedroom I shared with my brother. "And leave that hat up there. We don't wear hats in the house."

I didn't say anything else. I knew I had lost another battle. I felt angry and mixed up as I made my way up the stairs. Paulie followed me up to our room. I still had the hat on my head. I stared at myself in the mirror that was above the chest of drawers my brother and I kept our clothes in. My sister was right, damn her. I did look silly. Like a little boy playing dress up. I took the hat off and threw it against the wall.

"Don't do that," Paulie said, and ran across the room to pick it up. "I think it's a really cool hat. I wish I had one."

"Yeah. You can have it."

"Really?"

"Sure. Why not."

Paul put the hat on his head. Then walked over and looked in the mirror at himself and smiled. "I love this," he said, "but you need to keep it. It's your hat." He took it off and placed it carefully on top of the dresser. "You saved up for it and all."

"I don't want it," I said again. And then didn't say anything else. Just let the leather hat sit there.

Later that night I called George up on the phone to see how he was doing, but his mother said he couldn't talk then. When I saw him the next day in school, he didn't say anything about the red hat and I didn't say anything about mine.

Just a few months later George got hit by a car and was killed. It was the first time anybody I knew had died. I didn't know how to feel. I guess I was mostly just shocked. It was not something I ever imagined could happen. But then I never imagined that the pigeons would shit on his hat either. Or why George instead of me? Or why I couldn't talk to my parents? The whole damn thing was a mystery to me. And I sure never wore the motorcycle hat again.

A Day at the Ballpark with Dad

It was named Connie Mack Stadium. That's where the Philadelphia Phillies played; my hometown favorites, my heroes, the guys I wanted to grow up to be. Guys like Robin Roberts, Del Ennis, Granny Hamner; who played shortstop and who Dad said was "tough as nails." The big wad in Granny's cheek was chewing tobacco Dad told me. He was always spitting – Granny that is, not Dad. Dad smoked cigars as we sat in the stadium on those warm summer days. I was happy then. Maybe being at the ballpark with my dad and my brother Paul was as close to perfect as my life would ever be.

Sports were the only way and only time that I was able to connect with my father. In our regular day-to-day life he was distant, silent, sometimes threatening. Usually I tried to avoid him; Mom was always telling us not to "bother your father." Like he might explode if pushed the wrong way.

We would arrive at the ballpark early. And before the game we would go to a little hole in the wall soda fountain where Dad ordered us hot dogs with chili sauce, and chocolate cream sodas. I can't tell you with words how delicious that food was, unlike anything we ate at home. I *can* tell you how I felt about my father then. I thought he was perfect – strong, smart, even kind. I loved him. In a way I could never have spoken out loud.

Dad always got us good seats, down close to the field on the first base side. That would be the best place to catch a foul ball, Dad said, though we never did get one. Walking out from the dark tunnels into the bright interior of the stadium took my breath away. It was so big, so vivid, with the electric green outfield grass and the brown dirt of the infield, lovingly tended to by the grounds crew. Some of the players would already be out on the field taking batting practice. Someday, I told myself, I would be out there too, wearing a red, pinstriped Phillies uniform. I didn't tell Dad that, though. I was afraid he might have laughed at me and that would have ruined everything.

We'd buy scorecards before we got to our seats from a guy who hollered, "Get your pro-grammms here." Dad bought two, and gave one to me. Paul was still too young to know how to keep score, and didn't seem all that interested anyhow. Dad, though, had taught me how to do it – all the symbols and numbers you had to know to keep a running account of who had done what at each turn of bat. It was complicated, but I picked it up quickly because Dad expected me to, and because, well, because I wanted more than anything to please him.

Once the game got underway, we settled back into the hard wooden seats and became totally absorbed in the action on the field. Dad kept up a running commentary on the game, yelling encouragements at the Philly batters – "Come on, Richie. A little bingle. Let's get it going." Richie Ashburn was the leadoff hitter for the Phils and consistently had one of the best batting averages in the National League. Dad turned to me almost every time Ashburn came to the plate and said, "See, you don't have to be a slugger to be a great player." If Ashburn worked the count to three and two, Dad would yell out, "A walk's as good as a hit." There were dozens of these phrases he'd use, depending on the situation and who was at the plate. The other men in the seats around us were doing the same, whooping and yelling, and I would also join in, though my voice wasn't loud enough to be heard. Still it felt good, like I was part of something bigger than myself. Dad's loudest comments were reserved for the opposing team. He'd yell so loud I was sure the players could hear him. "No hitter, no hitter. This guy's a bum. Strike him out. Put it in his ear." This last I finally figured out to mean for our pitcher to hit the opposing batter in the head with the baseball. I don't think Dad meant that seriously. It was part of the game. We were all, us Philly fans, yelling and cheering together for the team. And when a Phillie player knocked one out of the ballpark for a homerun, we would all jump up as one body, screaming and stomping. Dad and I stood side by side clapping our hands as Willy "Puddinghead" Jones or catcher Stan Lopata or Elmer Valo circled the bases. If the home run put us ahead or won the game, maybe Dad even slapped me on the back. My little brother, Paul, cheered too, but I got the feeling that he was doing it just because everybody else was and as soon as he could he'd sit back down and continue eating roasted peanuts, the shells now scattered all under his seat.

By the ninth inning, I was tired and ready to leave. Including the drive over and all, we would have probably been gone for five hours or more. On the other hand, I really wasn't ready for the day at the park to end. I knew that once we left Connie Mack Stadium and got back in the car everything would go back to the way it was. Dad would stop talking, stop buying us treats. He'd drive us straight home, wouldn't look at me, and I, smart boy that I was, would also stop chattering, stop asking questions, stop being happy. And wait for the next day at the ballpark.

By the time I graduated from high school, Dad and I had stopped going to the games. We didn't have much to say to each other – not even about the Phillies. And once I left for college and continued on with my life, Dad and I grew even further apart. I imagined that he was angry that I had not followed in his footsteps to become a doctor, upset that I married a non-Jewish woman, disappointed that I had moved my family 3000 miles away from Philadelphia. Our days at Connie Mack Stadium were a distant memory.

Then in 1980 Mom and Dad came to visit us in

Seattle. Maybe because he was now retired, Dad seemed gentler, more open. He allowed my young daughters to climb onto his lap as he read them book after book. I bought us tickets to go see the Mariners play – good seats too, right on the first base side like Dad had taught me. We drank beer and ate peanuts and I kept score in the program. Dad still cheered and jeered at the action on the field. I did too. We shared the same vocabulary once again. Father and son.

Keeping Kosher

My mother hated Bubby. I didn't understand why. It made the air in our house heavy, like we were all moving through fog.

Bubby came to live with us after Zayde (my father's father) died, because she couldn't manage on her own. Zayde was the one who had taken care of all the interactions with the larger world. He went to work (as a tailor), paid the bills, talked to the American shopkeepers and neighbors. Bubby hid from all that, shuffling around in the small kitchen of their North Philadelphia apartment. She still dressed and acted like she was living in the shtetl, waiting for the Cossacks to return. I was a little kid at the time Bubby came to stay, but still I could sense that something big was up between my mother and father over Bubby's arrival. It was the only time I can remember seeing my dad cowed. It was as if he couldn't look my mother in the eye. He brought his mother to live with us, but he was ashamed of her immigrant ways. And fearful of my mother's outsized reaction.

I could never figure out why Mom was always so upset. Bubby didn't take up much space; she was a tiny, wizened woman who rarely spoke. She spent most of her days sitting in an old wingback chair reading the Yiddish edition of the Jewish Forward. She never did learn to read or write English, though she was able to write her name – Sara. My brother, Paul, and I would often ask her to show us, bringing her a pad and pencil, then marveling over her scrawly handwriting.

THE ATMOSPHERE AT HOME became more and more strained as the years went by. My mother was not a subtle woman, neither in affect or speech. She said what was on her mind and damn anyone who was in her way. Unfortunately, Bubby always seemed to be in the way. If we were all sitting in the living room watching the Ed Sullivan Show, Mom might jump up right in the middle and shout, "I can't relax with her in the room," staring at poor Bubby. And she'd keep right on standing there, hands on her hips, glaring now at Dad, until Bubby rose up out of her chair and shuffled off to her bedroom, hidden behind the kitchen. After Bubby was gone, Mom sat back down and we went on watching Topo Gigio or the guys spinning plates on sticks, but I felt awful, like I wanted to cry but knew that would get me in big trouble. I bet Dad felt the same.

Even though she seemed to be always sad, Bubby was the one I came to when things had gone badly for me at school or I had gotten into a fight with the

Catholic school kids in the neighborhood. She'd help me wash up and make me a snack of toast and tea. "You shouldn't worry," Bubby told me, "Some day you'll go to college, like your father." She made the word sound like coll-itch. I didn't ask her why going to coll-itch would make getting beat up any easier, but then she'd let me cry on her bony shoulder and she'd pat my head, smooth back my hair till I was done. Mom and Dad never touched me like that.

Bubby never pretended to be a modern American. How could she? She was an old-world Jew and she'd always kept kosher. I don't imagine it was something she had to think about. Mom, of course, did not keep a kosher house and made no secret of her annoyance at having to accommodate Bubby's dietary restrictions. "A bunch of superstitious nonsense," Mom announced every night at the dinner table as she slammed down Bubby's special plate. Bubby never answered back, just stared down at her food.

"Let my mother be," Dad said. You could tell he only wanted to eat his dinner and be gone, back to the peace of his downstairs doctor's office.

"You're not the one who has to cook for her," Mom snapped at him. When she talked about our grandmother Mom always made her into a pronoun, a her or a she or a 'this one.'

After we were done eating one night, Mom turned to Bubby and barked, "So? How'd you like your food?" We had eaten a stew full of potatoes and carrots and some sort of stringy meat.

"It was fine," Bubby said in her timid voice. "Very tasty."

"Tasty, huh?" Mom said, smirking. "Do you know what you ate?"

Bubby shook her head.

"Pig," Mom announced. "Nice juicy pork meat."

A silence descended over the table, each of us stunned or stricken. Even I knew enough about kosher food, to know that pork was the ultimate *treyf,* an unclean food. I felt like I might throw up.

Dad pushed his plate away and stood up, throwing his napkin down on the table. "That was uncalled for, Isabelle." He strode out of the dining room and we heard his footsteps descending the stairs. I wondered why he didn't try to console his mother, pat her shoulder, anything.

"It goes to show you," Mom said, after he left, "that those old rules don't mean a thing. Nothing's changed, has it?" She looked at Bubby. "You're still alive, aren't you?"

Bubby stood up. "You're a mean woman," she said, her voice swelling and breaking, "And God will punish you for this." Then she walked off to her bedroom and shut the door behind her.

Mom turned to me and my sister and brother. The air felt charged. My sick stomach was changing to something oddly approaching elation. My mom had done a horrible thing. But for once in our family's life, people were pushing back.

"Big deal," Mom said. I didn't know who she was speaking to. "I only wanted to show her what nonsense all that kosher stuff really is. We live in America, not Russia for God's sake." She sat back down and reached for her cigarettes.

"Can I be excused?" my little brother asked. Paul

was more sensitive than I was and I figured he would soon be sobbing into his pillow.

"Me too," my older sister Linda said. "I've got homework."

I gathered up my courage. Waited till Linda and Paul were gone. "You didn't have to do that," I said. "Bubby's right. You *are* really mean." Then I got up and walked into Bubby's room to see if I could make her feel any better, and left my mother alone at the table.

Uncle Jack – Who Worked at the Gas Station

"That Jack is a real card," my mother or father would say with a shake of the head and a half-smile, seeming to indicate that being a card was both a good and a bad thing. Clearly being a card would not be acceptable for most people, and certainly not for any of our repressed family unit, but with Jack, perhaps an exception could be made. "What are you gonna do," the other one would respond with a complementary shrug of the shoulders.

Mom and Dad were talking about my Uncle Jack, who wasn't actually my uncle, though we were directed to call him that. Uncle Jack was my Dad's first cousin, which made him my cousin also, but I guess it didn't sound right to call him Cousin Jack, and for sure kids didn't call adults by their first names. That would have been disrespectful. Whatever the name, I loved Uncle Jack. He was one of our only relatives who laughed and told jokes and stories, and, best of all, included the children in the conversation. When Uncle Jack came to visit, I felt like I'd been released from the gloomy silence our family lived in most of the time.

Uncle Jack was a big man, though not solid. He was fat, actually, and kind of sloppy looking. His shirt was always untucked and his trousers seemed in danger of falling down. His face was splotchy pink, but when he smiled or laughed he looked to me like one of the comedians we saw on television, Jimmy Durante or Jackie Gleason, someone I could both enjoy and admire.

"Put food in front of that Jack," Mom said, "and it's gone in thirty seconds." I think she too enjoyed our cousin, glad that someone openly appreciated her.

"Isabelle, you're the best," Uncle Jack would say, stuffing the little crackers with cream cheese and slices of lox into his mouth, crumbs tumbling down his shirtfront. "That Meyer is one lucky fella. Who wouldn't be in love with a woman like you." Mom may have even blushed at that, and she was not a woman easily given to embarrassment. Dad didn't say anything. Wouldn't even smile.

Uncle Jack worked at the Hess Gas Station across the river in Camden, New Jersey. When we drove down the Shore, Dad would stop there to fill up and Jack would lumber over wearing his Hess cap and shirt with his name stitched above the pocket. He'd pop his big head inside the back window and reach over and rub my head. "Butchie," he'd say. "How you doing, kiddo? How 'bout them Phillies?" But before I had a chance to answer, he'd pull back out and get the gas hose going and the windows squeegeed, all the while keeping up a running monologue directed at my dad who he called Meyer, not once, but over and over. "Meyer, let me tell you about this pain I've been having in my shoulder" and "You should see, Meyer, the look on Esther's face when I told her. Meyer, boychick, you wouldn't believe it." Meyer *was* my dad's first name, but no one ever called him that. It was always Dr. Freedman or 'Doc', or sometimes even 'sir.' Even Mom used his first name only in private, and then sparingly I imagine.

But Jack was not one to pay attention to formalities or social conventions, and, best of all I thought, he was never ashamed of who he was or what he did. "I work in a gas station," he said. "So big deal, I'm not about to get ulcers, am I? And you should see all the interesting people I meet." He'd put his beefy arm around my shoulder and bend down to speak right to my face, like we were best buddies. Except for Uncle Jack, I didn't know any other adults who treated me like I was a real person.

My other uncles, the real ones, acted like I was barely there, unless I happened to get in the way. My Uncle Milton even once told me to "Shut your mouth. No one wants to know what you think" when I dared to give voice at a family dinner to some opinion I had. Neither Mom or Dad spoke up to defend me. They kept right on eating, looking down at their dinner plates like they didn't even know me.

Jack would never have treated me like that. He even told me stories about when he and my father were kids and the crazy things they did: stealing candy, getting into fights, chasing pretty girls. One story that stuck with me was how my dad was the best musician in their group. He played the violin so well, Jack told me, that all the other kids – tough Jewish street kids – would beg him to play. I could hardly believe these stories were about the man who was my father. Dad sure never played music anymore.

As I got older, we saw less and less of Uncle Jack. I think my father told Mom not to invite him and Aunt Esther and their son Michael over to the house anymore. Though Dad had been tolerant of Uncle Jack's shenanigans, I overheard him say to Mom. "I don't have time for this anymore. All they want from me is free medical advice."

"The children like him," Mom said.

"The children don't know what they like," Dad said.

"I think they do," Mom said.

And then Dad didn't say anything cause he didn't have to.

But he's your cousin, I wanted to shout. And he's my favorite relative. But that's not the kind of thing you could get away with in our family. You didn't contradict my father; he wouldn't stand for it. I'd found that out the hard way.

Uncle Jack's son, Michael, who really was my cousin, was also a favorite. He and my brother Paulie and I would wrestle on the beach at the Shore, all twisted together in one sandy, sweaty, laughing pile of boys. Dad hadn't been able to bar Jack and Esther from our shore house. They never waited for an invitation, just showed up with a bag full of bagels and deli meats, and went out back to the outdoor shower to get into their swimsuits. On one occasion Jack, wearing his enormous bathing trunks, grabbed my sister's hula-hoop and right there in our living room began twirling it around his naked belly. We all fell on the floor in hysterics. "This is how Elvis does it," Jack shouted. "Look at me, I'm doing the twist."

Dad grumped around, trying to hide behind his copy of *The Philadelphia Inquirer,* but eventually gave in to Uncle Jack's non-stop banter and good cheer and put aside the paper and let Jack tell his stories, and sometimes I'd even catch Dad smiling or making a comment of his own. And I could imagine then Jack and Meyer as kids, running around the streets of South Philadelphia. I wanted badly to know this other man who was my father.

A few years later, Michael was diagnosed with leukemia. He was only thirteen at the time and after that blow, Jack was not as jolly as before. Michael, though, hung right in there and underwent all sorts of terrible medical treatments without complaining, even when all his hair fell out. I thought that he must have gotten his strength from being raised by such happy parents. But my parents rarely even smiled and I was healthy as a damn horse. None of it made sense.

Michael died when he was seventeen. At his funeral, Uncle Jack told me Michael had never even had a chance to have a girlfriend. Jack shook his head. He looked then almost like a different person. His face was pale and he'd lost a lot of weight. "It's just not right, is it, Butchie?"

I told him I was really sorry. I didn't know what else to say.

Don't Go in There

There were three of us that played together that year: Liz, me, and my little brother, Paulie. It didn't matter that Liz was a girl. She'd do anything that Paulie and I would. She was the first one to come up with the idea of knocking on the front door of the haunted house. "You do it, Butchie. You're the oldest."

"So what," I said. "That doesn't make any difference."

"You should," Paulie said. "Liz is right."

The house sat raised up on a full block of our West Philadelphia neighborhood. A massive old wooden building with white columns mounted on a sagging front porch and windows boarded up with planks of wood. It looked like it had been abandoned for years, like someone had walked out the door and left the house there to rot. It must have at one time been the home of very rich people, the kind of people who didn't live around here anymore. I knew from overhearing my parents talk that lots of people had left and moved to the suburbs where it was supposed to be much nicer. And safer. My mom and sister wanted us to move there too, though we never did. Dad didn't think it was right to move just because some different kinds of people were coming in to the neighborhood. He said, "Right here is fine." And that was the end of it. A few years later Liz's family went off to Bryn Mawr.

I don't remember why we decided the old mansion was haunted. Maybe we heard it from other kids. We were sure there was somebody or something living inside of there, but so far we had been too scared to go and see. We had ventured as far as the front lawn, darting up, then running breathlessly back to the corner, safely outside of the reach of the ghosts inside.

Now Lizzie and my brother were pushing for more, as long as they didn't have to be the ones to chance it. Since at nine years old, I had one year on Liz and two over Paulie, I felt I had no choice. I didn't want them to call me chicken and make those clucking noises. "Go ahead," Liz said again. "Come on. You've got to." Her cheeks were pink with excitement as she bounced up and down on her toes. I think I was half in love with her, though I didn't then know anything about love or much about girls.

"Do it, do it, do it," Paulie chanted, hopping in time with Liz, the two of them in league against me, as I often imagined they were. I remember how they held hands, how they laughed together, how they seemed to share one mind. Different from mine. They needed me to be brave for them, to go ahead, but I suspected that they would rather play without me. And often they did just that.

"You two are such little sissies," I said. "You're scared of everything."

"I dare you," Liz said. "I double dare you." She had dark hair cut in a pageboy, like Prince Valiant and big white teeth, like Chiclets.

"You two will probably run away when I go up there."

"Will not," Liz said, and stared over at Paulie to bring him into line.

"I promise," he said, trying to look serious.

I took a deep breath and squatted down. The other two followed my lead and did the same. Now we were safely hidden from whoever was inside the haunted house. This was the part I liked. They would do whatever I told them. I was the boss, just like my dad was at home. "Okay, here's the plan." I looked at each of them in turn, like I was sizing them up and deciding who should do what, but really I was stalling for time. "Be quiet, I don't want them to hear us."

"I am being quiet," Paulie said, "I didn't say anything."

"Tell us what to do," Lizzie said. I could see her skinned knees now. Liz's mom made her wear homemade dresses to school, so she was always getting scraped up on the hard asphalt schoolyard where we played tag.

"You two have to create a distraction. That's the only way I'll do it."

"What does dis-tractashun mean?" Paulie asked.

"He means like in the movies," Liz said. "Like when the deputy fires his gun at the bad guy while the sheriff sneaks up from behind."

"Yeah, I don't want them to see me coming."

"Who's them?" my brother said. I could tell he was getting nervous. Paulie was still too young to pretend to be brave. He tried to stand up, but I reached over and pulled him back down.

"Owww. Don't!" He batted my hand away, but plunked back down on to his knees.

"They're going to see you," I hissed.

"You're crazy," Paulie said. "There's nobody there anyway. It's just pretend."

"No," Lizzie said, and put her arm around Paulie's shoulder. "I've seen them."

He looked like he was about to cry. "When?"

"Lots of times," Liz said. ""You can see them peeking out when they think no one is looking."

"It's true," I said. "They're inside. " And at the moment I believed what I said.

"Are you really gonna do it?" Paulie said.

"I guess so," I said, hoping there was still a way out.

"We have to now," Liz said. Her eyes looked as big as half dollars.

I knew I had to make a move. "Okay, so you and Paulie have to go first."

"I'm not going first," he chirped. "Unh uh."

"You don't have to go to the front door, dummy, I'm doing that part."

"Don't call him that," Liz said, easing closer to my little brother.

"Okay, but you have to do what I tell you. Run across the grass, away from the house."

"That's like the part in the movies, right?" Lizzie asked. "The *distraction* part." I could tell she was excited and that made me feel more excited too.

"Yeah, so I can run up to the front door without them seeing me."

"Remember, you have to knock on the door. Loud," Liz said.

"I know what I'm doing," I snapped.

"What if they try to come after us?" Paulie wanted to know.

"Don't worry," I told him. "You'll be able to run faster."

"You sure?"

"I'm sure, dum-dum."

"Butchie, don't," Liz warned, sounding bossy like my mother.

"Let's do this already," I said.

"Okay," Paulie said quietly.

"Okay then, " Liz said and held out her hand, palm down. I put my hand on top of hers. Her skin felt warm and smooth. Paulie added his hand to ours, and together we nodded and said, "Fuckaduck." It was something we'd heard the older kids say and had made it our secret word, our agreement to be brave.

I pulled my hand out of the pile and clenched my jaw. "Go on, then." I pointed to the cracked concrete steps that led up to the front yard.

Lizzie stood and pulled Paulie after her. Then she smiled at me in a funny sort of way, like she hadn't ever done before. "This is going to be great." Then she was gone, rushing up the steps with Paulie right on her tail. They were still holding hands, running as if stray dogs from the neighborhood were chasing them.

I waited ten seconds, as much as I could stand, then dashed up the steps myself. At the top I halted and looked around. Liz and Paulie were streaking across the dirt lot, away from the house. I could hear them giggling. That made me mad. They were having all the fun. As usual. My head swiveled to the haunted house. I could feel my heart pounding against my ribs. I moved along the flagstone path that led to the front of the porch. All I have to do, I told myself, is knock on the door and run like crazy.

The old house shimmered in front of me, like it was a live thing. The wide front porch was cluttered with rolled up newspapers and empty glass milk bottles. Then a voice called out from inside, low and muffled. "Who's there?"

I couldn't believe my ears. I wanted to turn around and run, but I couldn't move. The voice called out again. "What do you want here?"

I knew I wouldn't be able to speak if I tried. My mouth felt like it was full of glue. My legs were shaking. I thought that only happened in cartoons. With a last burst of courage, I raced to the front door and raised my fist to knock.

That's when the door swung open. I felt like I'd stuck my finger in an electric wall socket. My mouth gaped open, and I stared at the person standing there in the doorway. Too shocked to even yell, I felt a warm trickle run down my leg.

"What do you want here?"

I continued to stare.

"You know how to talk, don't you? All you do is open your mouth and let the words come out." Then she started laughing. It was a familiar sound and allowed me to take a breath and figure out that I probably wasn't going to die and that the old woman standing in the doorway wasn't a monster or a ghost, at least not like any I'd imagined.

"My brother and my girlfriend dared me," I finally squeaked out and instantly felt my face flush. Why had I called Lizzie my girlfriend?

"Shouldn't let your friends push you into things you don't want to do," she said. Her voice sounded normal, like an old Jewish lady. Her hair was gathered on top of her head in a gray bun held in place by a hairnet. She had on a couple of sweaters, though it wasn't a cold day. She looked a little bit like my grandmother, the one who moved here from Poland and still spoke with an accent that Paulie and I sometimes made fun of. "Now look, boychick," she pointed to the front of my pants. "You've gone and wet yourself. What's your mother going to say about this?"

"I don't know." I tried to cover up the stain with my hands. "My mom's not home yet. She works."

"Good for her," the old woman said, gazing out over my shoulder. "So, where is this brother and girlfriend of yours?"

"She's not really my girlfriend. We just play together. A lot."

"She's a friend and she's a girl. That makes her your girlfriend. Don't worry so much."

"Okay," I said, wondering how she knew that I was always worried about stuff.

"You tell her to come over here." She rubbed her bony hands together, like she was trying to warm them.

"They won't come. They're too scared."

"What's to be scared?" She smiled so that all the

creases in her face moved into a new arrangement. She didn't have a strong accent like my grandmother, but she smelled the same, like old library books and baby powder.

"We thought this house was haunted," I confessed.

"Haunted, eh? That's a good one." She coughed, a dry sound like leaves crunching underfoot. "Tell them it's okay. Nothing haunted about this place except my memories." I wasn't sure what she meant, so just shrugged. "Go on now." She pushed me lightly on the shoulder. I could barely feel her touch, but I realized in that moment that I wasn't scared any more.

I walked to the edge of the porch and called out to where Liz and Paulie were hiding. "Come on over. Everything's okay." My voice didn't shake or anything and I felt good, like I'd just hit the ball over the roof in a stickball game. "It's just an old lady."

It took another minute, but finally I saw them moving slowly back across the raggedy patch of weeds that used to be the front lawn. Liz was leading the way, with Paulie two steps behind, looking like he might dart away at any second. "She wants us to come inside," I called out.

"Really?" Liz said. "Inside of there?"

"Yeah, it's okay," I said. "She's nice. Come on." Then I remembered the stain on the front of my pants and tried to turn away.

"You peed yourself," Paulie said, but he wasn't laughing. I thought he sounded worried, like I'd stepped on a nail or something.

"It's nothing," I said, not able to look at them. I turned back to the porch. The old lady was still standing in the doorway. She waved her hand.

"Is she one of the ghosts?" Paulie said.

"There aren't really ghosts," Liz said to him, then turned to me. "Are there, Butchie?"

"Nope," I said. "She's a real person. Jewish I think. Now come on, we can get to see the inside."

"I don't want to," Paulie said. "I wanta go home now."

"Don't be a baby," I said.

"I'm not a baby."

Liz grabbed his hand. "We'll go for a little while, then we can leave if you want."

"Let's go." I turned around and led them up the broken steps. No one said a word.

"Don't worry, I'm not gonna bite," the old lady said, grinning and looking us over. "I can tell you two are brothers. Cut from the same bolt of cloth you are." Then she settled her gaze on Liz and smiled so that I could see she had a cracked front tooth. "Now aren't you the little darling," she said and patted Lizzie's smooth black hair. "Gonna be a real heartbreaker."

"Thank you, ma'am," Liz said. I'd never heard her call anybody ma'am before. It sounded silly and I burst out laughing. Both Liz and the old lady gave me a dirty look.

"So who wants cookies and milk?" she asked.

"I do," Paulie said quickly. He didn't look so worried anymore.

"Okay, I guess," I said. We followed the old lady into the darkness of our former haunted mansion, now just an old beat up house with an old lonely lady.

Over stale sugar cookies and milk, she told us that she was the sister of the rich guy who used to own the place. Turns out he hadn't run off to the suburbs, he'd just died and left the place to the old woman, who told us her name was Sadie Rosenberg and that if we wanted to, we could call her Aunt Sadie. I didn't say anything, but didn't see any good reason to call her Aunt, no matter how nice she was.

Sadie told us that she didn't have much money and so when the neighborhood kids started throwing rocks through her windows, all she could do was nail boards up over the broken glass. I think we all felt kind of guilty then. Not because we were the ones who threw the rocks, but because we knew that those kids were probably playing like it was a haunted house too.

Lizzie said, after we'd eaten all the cookies, "Why don't you sell this house, then you could move somewhere nicer."

"I'm too far gone for all that," Sadie said. "Don't know how I'd go about it."

"We'd better get going," I interrupted. I was thinking about my still damp trousers and getting home before Mom did.

"We don't have to go yet," Paulie said. "It's still early."

"Is not," I said, shooting him a look that promised a punch on the arm.

"I could come back tomorrow, Aunt Sadie, to visit," Lizzie said. "If you want."

"Oh, that would be lovely, sweetheart," Sadie said. A smile spread across her face. But she also seemed like she was about to cry. Her shoulders trembled like leaves on a tree.

I didn't understand how people could be like that. Happy and sad at the same time. But there were a lot of things I didn't get then. Half the time I felt like I was stumbling around in the dark, trying not to bump into the walls. All I knew was that tomorrow or the next day, Lizzie and my little brother were probably going to come back and visit this old woman, without me. That was the way it was going to happen and I had better get used to it. I would be on the outside looking in at them eating sugar cookies and laughing.

"Come on, let's get out of here," I said. "It's getting late."

Part Two

Adolescent Angst

Down the Shore

The anticipation was almost as exciting as the arrival. My brother and I could barely contain ourselves as the school year drew to a close. "Pretty soon," we'd tell each other in strained voices, "we'll be down the Shore."

"I'm not gonna wear shoes all summer long," I said.

"You will when the sand gets really hot," Paul said, "or else you'll burn your feet like you did last summer."

"Did not," I said.

"Did so," Paulie said.

Going to the New Jersey coast was the time that all of our family seemed to live for. It was both a release and a relief from the tedium of our everyday life in hot, gritty Philadelphia. At first we went down for only one week, the next summer – two, then for a couple more years, a month in the upstairs apartment of a family friend. Each year was better than the one before. I loved swimming in the ocean and body surfing. I liked being brave, plunging into the big waves, even when it meant getting knocked around and pulled under into a whirlwind of pounding water. Most of all I loved how free I felt at the beach, wearing nothing all day but a bathing suit, the sun hot on my bare back.

Then one day in May Dad sat down at the dinner table and announced that he had bought us a house at the Shore.

"What do you mean?" Mom asked. "You bought a house?"

"I couldn't pass it up," he said. "From one of my patients. She's retiring and can't keep the place up anymore. She's practically giving it away. So I told her I'd buy it. Gave her a check right then and there. We'll go down this week-end to look at it." I was amazed. That was the longest speech I'd ever heard from my dad.

"And you did all this without saying a word to me?" Mom said. She sounded angry and I was afraid they were going to have a big fight about it right there at the table. I was holding my breath. But then I saw Mom's shoulders relax, a half-smile crossed her face. "So, it's a nice place?" she asked.

"I think so," Dad said. "It's got an outdoor shower."

"Cool," I yelped, but didn't go on when Dad shot me a look.

"You have to go outside to shower?" my sister Linda whined.

"There's one inside also," Dad said.

"That's good," Mom said.

"Okay, then," Dad said. "Let's eat."

Underneath the table I punched my brother in the leg. I was so happy I could barely eat the meatloaf and lumpy mashed potatoes Mom passed around the table. But I did.

THE HOUSE, A COTTAGE really, was everything we hoped for. The first thing I noticed when we pulled up in front was the shutters. They were painted black with white wooden cutouts of naked mermaids tacked on them. (Turned out the house was on Mermaid Avenue. Seriously.) The cottage had two bedrooms on the main floor – one for Mom and Dad, the other for my sister, who was now in high school and acted all superior. Paulie and I had the whole upstairs, which was essentially an unfinished attic with a couple of iron bed frames with sagging mattresses. We loved it. That attic felt like our own private world, and if we brought down our dirty laundry and didn't make too much noise, Mom was unlikely to climb the narrow staircase to yell at us.

My dad only came down the Shore on weekends. During the week he stayed in Philadelphia to keep office hours, then would drive down on Friday nights. Each week I dreaded my father's arrival. Once he showed up, the entire atmosphere of the place changed. Everybody became stiffer. Even the air inside the house felt heavier. No more laughing or loud talking, no more eating at the picnic table outside. Dad didn't think it was proper, to be on display like that. At least that's what Mom said he thought. She was always telling us all kinds of things that Dad thought. Maybe they weren't even true. How could I know?

"Shit," I said to my brother as we were walking back from the beach on a hot Friday afternoon. "I don't know why he comes down at all. The fucker doesn't even go in the ocean."

"You shouldn't curse," Paulie said. "It's not right."

"Screw you, momma's boy." I punched him on the shoulder. He was eleven, I was almost fourteen, but the gap between us seemed wider this summer. I was no longer willing to be a good boy. Sometimes I felt like I was going to explode with all the feelings I couldn't quite name or understand.

I knew Mom was just waiting for Dad to arrive so she could report to him all the ways I'd been "fresh" to her all week and how I'd been coming home late in the evenings. Late to Mom meaning any time after eight pm. I'd been hanging out with a new group of friends, boys and girls both, and sometimes we'd even drink cans of warm beer and make out on the beach.

As soon as my father arrived that week, before he'd even settled into his special chair, Mom was all over him. "I hope you're going to talk to that boy." She hovered around him in the cottage's tiny living room.

Dad was trying to get himself settled, pulling off his tie, rolling up the cuffs of his long-sleeved white shirt, kicking off his shoes. Tomorrow he'd put on his droopy bathing shorts, a terry-cloth shirt, and his black-billed captain's hat. I guess the Shore was his place to relax also. If Mom would only let him.

"What boy are you talking about, Isabelle?"

I was slouched down on one end of the couch; Paulie was at the other end. It was where we were supposed to be when Dad arrived. "You need to greet your father," Mom told us. "He works hard all week so you can spend your summers here. It's the least you can do."

"Which boy?" Mom chirped. "Which boy is it always?"

Dad was finally able to get past her and fall into his easy chair with an audible sigh. "What is your mother talking about?" He looked right at me for the first time.

"I don't know."

"You don't know?" Dad said.

"He knows," Mom said.

"Do not," I said.

"You certainly do," Mom said.

"No I don't."

"That's enough, dammit," Dad yelled. "You'd think I could have one minute of peace and quiet, one minute to relax."

"I've got these kids all week," Mom said. "How do you think I feel?"

"All you do is sit on the beach and play *Password* with your friends," I said, just loud enough to be heard.

"You see how he talks to me?" Mom said.

Dad sighed, reached for his pipe. "Don't be fresh to your mother," he said without much conviction. Dad needed a shave and his eyes were red rimmed behind his eyeglasses. I kinda felt sorry for him.

"Okay, I won't talk fresh to her anymore. Can we watch television now?"

"Yeah," Paulie said, "*The Fugitive* is on."

Dad took off his glasses and rubbed his eyes. "Fine," he said. "Fine."

"No television," Mom said, looking at Dad. "Someone needs to learn some manners around here."

"No fucking way," I said. There was a deep silence immediately after those three words escaped my mouth.

"What did he say?" Dad sat forward in his chair, putting the pipe aside.

"I told you," Mom said, looking oddly pleased.

"I want to know what he said," Dad commanded.

Paulie broke the silence. "He said, 'No fucking way'. I told him he shouldn't curse."

I couldn't believe my brother had betrayed me, but I had no time to respond, because Dad was rising out of his chair now. I jumped up off the couch, maybe to run, maybe to defend myself. I don't know because almost as soon as I got to my feet and opened my mouth, my father's big hand exploded across the side of my head and I collapsed in a heap on the floor. "Don't you ever talk back to me," Dad said in a strangled voice.

"I didn't," I managed to squeak out from down on the ground.

I was angry and humiliated, but I wasn't scared anymore. I even had an urge to laugh, and I probably would have said something else, but my mother rushed over and knelt down beside me. "That's enough now," she said, looking at me and not my father, like I was the one who had hit somebody.

Dad still stood above me with his hands clenched at his side. Then he let out a deep breath, almost a sob. He turned away and went back to his chair, sat down, and picked up the newspaper.

Mom put her hand on mine like she was going to help me up, but I pushed it away and stood up on my own. I felt tears running down my cheeks, but I didn't cry out loud. I looked over at my dad, but he wouldn't look back at me. I turned away and went upstairs and lay on my bed, staring up at the unfinished ceiling. It was like I wasn't even in my body; I couldn't feel a thing.

When Paulie came up to go to bed a couple hours later, he said, "I'm sorry, Butchie. I didn't think he would hit you like that. Really."

I didn't answer him. There was nothing left to say. I knew I was through with all of them.

Jew Bunny – Part 1

I've always felt confused about being a Jew. Not that I didn't know I was one. That part was always pretty clear, even as a kid, though I don't remember anyone specifically saying to me, "You are a Jew, Robert." And certainly my parents never said, "You're a Jew and here's what that means." I wonder what they would have told me. But my parents were not that kind of Jew. Just what kind they were took me much longer to figure out.

My mom used to say to me, "You're so handsome; you don't look Jewish at all." I was both flattered and, here's that word again, confused. "You're a good looking boy, with those blue eyes and dirty blonde hair."

"Jews don't have dirty blonde hair?"

"Or blue eyes either."

"So where did mine come from?"

"You ask too many questions," Mom said. "It's a problem with you."

Of course, I pieced some idea of Jewishness together, like kids do. Mom not only thought I was handsome (Good). But also thought Jews were ugly, and maybe even a bit, I don't know, coarse (Bad). Like my friends, Joey Cohn and Gary Earlbaum. I guess both of those guys were ugly and their mothers probably never told them they were handsome. Gary had a big honker of a nose, that curved down almost to his upper lip. They both had dark curly hair and olive colored skin. I didn't know they were ugly until I'd had that conversation with my mother. And then I figured out that all the Jewish kids in my school were not very good to look at and would be that way all their lives, except maybe some of the girls who would get nose jobs to straighten out their big Jew noses. At the same time, I began to notice that the gentile kids were mostly pretty good looking, especially the girls, with their long, straight blonde hair and nice way of talking, not all nasally and loud like the Jewish girls. Mom said, "You can always tell who's a Jew. Even with your eyes closed."

There were also kids at my school who didn't fit either category. The black kids were a group all to themselves. I had a few black friends, but not too many, and, truthfully, not very close ones. This seemed mutually agreed upon. We'd ignore them and they'd ignore us. Then there were the Italian kids, who looked sort of Jewish, but were Christian. So that was also kind of puzzling. My other good buddy was named Charley Kapeghian, who looked like Joey and Gary, but Charley said he was Armenian. Mom said that was not so good either. Then she said, "Don't go around talking about people's nationalities. It's not a good idea."

"Why not?"

"It's not polite. These are things you keep to yourself. Especially now."

"Why? What's going on now?"

"You'll know when you're older," she said, which is something she said a lot. It always made me mad when she did and so almost every conversation I had with her I would end up steaming and dismissed to my room to take my frustrations out on my little brother, who didn't understand why I always wanted to wrestle with him.

I also couldn't tell what my father thought about being Jewish. It's not something he ever spoke about. He wasn't an "observant Jew." He didn't go to synagogue, unless there was some special occasion – a bar mitzvah or a wedding. Or sometimes we went to services on Yom Kippur, which is the most important Jewish high holy day, and when we did Dad would bring along his tallit bag, a small purple velvet pouch, with Hebrew letters stitched on the outside, and when we got to the shul, he would take out the tallit and put it on in this very formal way while muttering some words and kissing each corner of the long silk shawl. So, I figured he knew something about all this Jewish stuff that he wasn't telling me about. I asked him, "When do I get a tallit?"

"When you're bar mitzvahed," he muttered.

So maybe they would all let me in on the secret at that point, I figured.

And then there were my grandparents, Dad's parents. They were religious. In an old-fashioned way. They even went to a synagogue that was way more strict than our conservative place. My grandparents' shul was Orthodox. I only went there with them a couple of times, which was fine with me. It wasn't much fun for a kid; the services droned on for hours. I remember that Bubby had to sit upstairs, in a little balcony, separated from the men who sat downstairs in front of the Ark, and who said all the prayers and kept jumping up and down and bowing and chanting. I didn't get what any of it meant. Bubby and Zayda were no help. Bubby barely spoke English, but she was a good cook and I liked going over to their dark little apartment where all Bubby wanted to do was fill me full of stuffed cabbage and cluck over me, which was all fine, but, you know, confusing. Why did they act like they were still living in some other country, or like they were hiding? In their apartment there were always heavy drapes pulled across the windows. I wish I had been smart enough to ask questions then. I bet Bubby and Zayda would have answered my questions or tried to. My first one would have been: "What makes someone a Jew?" My second question would have been, "Is it something you get to decide about yourself?" And then I might have asked, "So, why don't people like us?"

I should say that this initial period of confusion about my Jewishness occurred during the 1950's. Which, looking back, was an unusual time period for many different reasons. Of course, I didn't know any of those reasons then, and just stumbled along as best I could, which probably is what Mom and Dad were doing also. The fifties were like that, the "don't rock the boat" decade. Everything's fine. Really.

Now I realize that my parents' experience was shaped by the depression in the 30's and by World

War II, and especially by what happened to the Jews in Europe during that war. My dad had served in the Army Air Corps overseas, yet he never once mentioned anything about all that horrible shit that happened to the Jews over there. If he told any war stories at all, which I might have overheard, they were about the sights he'd seen in Egypt and India and other places he'd been sent as a doctor, but he made it all sound almost like a vacation, a sightseeing trip. Once I heard my Uncle Jack, who'd also been over there, ask my dad about "the camps." "What was it like, Meyer, when you got there?" but Dad just shook his head to show that wasn't something he would talk about. I didn't even know about the holocaust until I was in high school. Even Bubby and Zayda never said anything about what happened "over there." Maybe it was all just too painful. Or they thought, this isn't something kids should hear. Which does make some kind of sense, and I can only imagine what I would have made of hearing about gas chambers and exterminations, and Jews in small towns having to dig their own graves, old people and kids too. I was horrified when I finally did learn about it, as anybody would be, but by then it felt distant; I didn't understand all the connections. Didn't understand that it was my tribe, my people, parts of my family who had suffered and died there. Just because they were Jews.

Dad was busy being a doctor with a family practice and Mom was the doctor's wife, a role she was clearly proud of. Though I didn't know the word then, they were assimilating. Mom said that we (children) shouldn't act like Jew Bunnies. I thought that was pretty funny, imagining little rabbits bouncing around with yarmulkes on their bunny heads. We always had to be careful to speak well (which meant speaking like upper-crust gentiles, like the people on TV), be dressed nicely, not be "pushy", and never seem like we were in any way greedy or tight with our money.

I couldn't make sense out of what it meant to be a Jew, but the questions were always in my head, nibbling away. On the one side, I was led to believe that Jews were smart, smarter than gentiles, and successful. From early on, I was told that I was going to be a doctor like my father. And all my (male) cousins were also expected to be doctors or lawyers, or, failing that, C.P.A's. Jews didn't drive trucks or work with tools; leave that to the goyim. The other side of the equation, though, had us as inferior in all-important ways to the Christian world – status, attractiveness, likeability. More than once I'd been called a "dirty Jew." And then there'd be a fight.

My bar mitzvah, as it approached, only further muddied the Jewish waters for me. Before I could go through with the ritual, I had to go to Hebrew School, to prepare, and, supposedly, to learn about our history and language and about the Torah, the Jewish bible. I had been looking forward to it, but the reality turned out to be quite gloomy and joyless. We met in the musty smelling upstairs classrooms of Congregation Beth El, which was at 58th and Walnut Street. I had to take a long bus ride there after getting out of my regular public school classes. It made for a tiring day. This went on for a full year before my 13th birthday, when I was to magically become a man. It didn't work on any count. I didn't learn Hebrew, (though I still can sound out the letters), and I didn't much care about the Old Testament bible stories, which seemed like mean spirited fairy tales. And I didn't have a clue about who this *Adonai* guy was supposed to be, unless He was some super-charged version of my own father. All-powerful, vengeful, always ready and willing to reign down His wrath on anybody who crossed Him.

Still, I was basically a good boy, so I kept going to Hebrew school classes and as the time got closer to the assigned date of my bar mitzvah, I began the tedious preparation for the actual ceremony. This included memorizing a long portion of the Torah in Hebrew, which I would chant on the day of my bar mitzvah, and then be feted at a big party that my mother was already furiously planning. Things were starting to feel crazy, and I was not one whit closer to understanding what it really meant to be Jewish. I even went so far as to ask the Rabbi, when I went to meet with him so he could check my progress on learning my haftorah.

"Rabbi Morris," I said, "I don't get what all of this means?"

"All of what?" Rabbi Morris had an untrimmed black beard and if you looked closely, you could see food crumbs stuck in there. He always wore a black kippah, and his office smelled like old books and rubbing alcohol.

"You know, this Jewish stuff. Just because I get Bar Mitzvahed, does that mean I'm a full-fledged Jew."

"I guess you could call it that. It was different in the old days." He stared up at the ceiling. I followed his gaze, but didn't see anything up there. "Times change," he muttered. "What are you gonna do?" He held his palms up, like he was asking for something. I didn't know what. "Okay already, let's hear your portion."

So I would stumble through my haftorah, and Rabbi Morris would sit back and listen, and eventually I had it all memorized, and the big day arrived, and never had I felt more alienated from being a Jew than I did then. I was just bright enough to see through all the hypocrisy and pretense, though not yet smart enough to pick out what could have been truly meaningful. I sensed, somewhere deep down, that the rituals I was participating in, taking the Torah out of the Ark, standing with the elders of the synagogue, wearing the tallit, did have meaning. But all I could focus on was that I had better do a good job, so my mother wouldn't be embarrassed in front of all the family and friends she had invited. And then I'd better be a pleasant host, Mom warned, at the lavish party to be held in a local ballroom that evening, where all sorts of people I barely knew would congratulate me on becoming a man, and pass me envelopes with money in them. "Give those to your father," Mom said.

That night Dad looked even less happy than I was, but Mom was prancing around like Queen Esther herself, wearing her new dress that had a collar made of "real mink." Looked to me like a dead squirrel. But as Mom told me more than once during the lead up to that party, I was "an ungrateful and self-centered boy." She was probably right. But I still didn't like her dress or her party, and the following week I told Rabbi Morris that I wouldn't be continuing in Hebrew school. He didn't seem surprised. My parents didn't care either.

High School Sucks

I am 14 and have just entered Central High School – an all-boys public school that is a long subway ride away from my neighborhood. Nothing is familiar anymore and nobody knows who I am. The juniors and seniors look to me like full-grown men – some of them even have scraggly beards. I'm still a long way from shaving or from anything else that might signal manhood. I want to be invisible – but soon learn that will not be possible. The seniors are all over us, taunting and teasing. Sometimes pushing and punching. The smaller, weak-looking boys get the worst of it. Everybody seems okay with it, even the teachers, like it's some sort of funny game.

During phys. ed. class, I get my first real taste of the hazing. Gym classes are all mixed together, freshmen, sophomores, juniors and seniors. Today we are playing softball on a hard-packed dirt field, and I'm feeling pretty good about the game. I've already gotten two singles, and am now at bat for my third time. I've always been good at sports. I hit the first pitch deep to left field and start running, head down. The left fielder has to chase the ball all the way to the fence by which time I'm rounding third and heading home, my team cheering me on. As I get close to the plate the catcher, a heavy-set senior boy, stands up to block my path and I have no choice but to run smack into him. I go down, scraping my leg across the rocky dirt. The catcher barely budges. Just stands there above me, grinning, waiting for the ball to finally get to him so he can tag me out. Fuck him, I think, and scramble to my feet to try and tag home. The asshole pushes me aside, but then some guys on my team run out and push him away and I score the run. As I head back to the side of the field, I look down at my leg and see below my white gym shorts, that my whole leg is scraped up and bleeding. It looks like a hunk of raw steak. I almost start crying, but catch myself. High school boys do not cry. But the fat catcher has already seen the look in my eye, and grins. "Hey, come here, frosh," he says to me. "Let me take a look at that." And then when I walk over to him, he bends over, grabs up a handful of dirt and gravel and tosses it at my cut up leg. The gravel sticks all over the wound, caught up in the blood. "There, that'll fix it," he says. A bunch of the other boys start laughing.

I don't know what the hell to do. He's way too big to fight. And nobody else seems to give a shit, so I just walk away again, and sit down on the bench. I start picking the gravel out of my leg.

THE NEXT TIME I have to deal with this hazing stuff is with my friend Paul Blaze. Well, he's sort of my friend. It's more like I've decided to look out for him. Paul is this very smart kid, who doesn't have the first clue about how to act around other kids. Maybe it's because he's skinny, and stutters, so he's been picked on probably his whole school life. And, to top it off, he looks like a little old man. His hair is thin on top, he walks stooped over, and he wears coke-bottle thick glasses. Now here he is at Central High School, which is supposed to be this big deal, where only the smartest kids from around the city are admitted. And Paul thought that maybe here, for once, he'd be safe. But Central is just as bad, if not worse, than any regular high school when it comes to teasing and bullying. Maybe it's because without any girls around, the boys don't feel like they have to hold anything back.

"I don-don-don-don't know what to do," Paul says to me. "Wha-wha-why won't they la-la-leave me alone?" We're in the same Latin class during third period, and since Paul and I are the only ones to answer any of Dr. Sandstrom's questions, we naturally start hanging out together. I felt kinda sorry for him, but I didn't know what to tell him. I was having my own problems. Unlike Paul, I wasn't at all sure I was really smart enough to be at Central. I'd never had to study before. Didn't even know how to do it, but knew that if I didn't I'd be booted out. And my parents would be VERY disappointed in me. My mother had already told me as much. "I expect you to be on the honor roll, Butch. If you want to get into medical school, you need to get all A's."

Paul Blaze, though, he's a damn genius. He's already taking college algebra and physics. He helps me with my geometry. It all comes easy for him, but he explains the problems carefully, so as not to make me feel stupid. I like Paul for that.

"Just be cool," I finally tell him. "You can't act like you're scared or they'll just keep messing with you. It's like when a dog knows you're scared of it."

"What is?" Paul is looking more pasty today than usual.

"The dog, man. If it knows you're scared, it barks louder, and maybe even bites your ass."

"I ca-ca-ca-ca-can't act like I'm suh-something I'm not."

"Yeah, you can. Everybody has to do it. Nobody's who they really are."

Paul looks doubtful. "I've got, got.., an idea," he says.

"Okay. I can't stand the suspense. Tell me."

"No, you'll have to wa-wa-wait and see."

"How long?"

"Till tomorrow," Paul says, and smiles for the first time in as long as I've known him.

When I first see Paul the next day, I know something is out of whack. He is twenty feet ahead of me in the basement corridor where we have our lockers. There is a whole crowd of kids around him and I can hear a lot of excited jabbering. I hurry to catch up, and push my way through the circle of mean-faced boys. Paul won't even look at me when I get next to him; it feels like he doesn't even notice me. He is bent over at the waist, even more so than usual, and his right hand is stuck out in front of him, belt high and is making a continual circular motion, and there's some sort of odd squawking noise going on, like static from a radio. I can't tell where it's coming from, especially with all the noise from the surrounding boys.

"Paul, what the hell is going on?" I say. But he won't look at me. He's moving ahead at a very slow pace, the hand going round and round, first finger pointing down. Then one of the boys gives Paul a hard push on the shoulder. Paul squeals, a terrible sound, though not one that seems to come from pain. In fact, Paul's expression has not changed one bit. I grab the boy who has pushed Paul and spin him around. "Cut it out," I yell. "Leave him the fuck alone."

"I'm not doing anything," the kid says. "He wants us to push him. It knocks the needle off the track." All the boys laugh. And before I can stop him, another kid pushes Paul. He stumbles forward and the squealing noise comes again. This time I think I recognize what it sounds like. I try to get Paul's attention, and grab his arm. Out comes the squeal, metallic and loud.

"Hey, you knocked the needle off the record," a kid with a shock of red hair tells me.

"Yeah, man," another kid says, "Don't you like music?" Then he pushes Paul's arm and I watch as it skitters back and forth, like the needle arm on an old fashioned record player. When his arm settles back into position, Paul keeps walking, bent over, and making the staticy sound, which I now realize is supposed to be like classical music. All the boys are following him down the hall, laughing, and pushing him along and shouting.

"Hey Paul, play Elvis."

"You gotta put a quarter up his ass if you want music."

"What a retard."

It's a terrible thing, like my friend is being attacked by a pack of hyenas. I can't take it anymore and run after them, and grab Paul out of their circle, dragging him away towards an empty classroom. He is squealing like a pig now, or I guess the record is squealing. The boys are yelling at me to leave him alone. Like I'm the one who's torturing him.

When I get Paul into the classroom and slam the door closed behind us, I turn to him. He still won't look at me and stays bent over, doing the dumb ass thing with his right hand, making the squeaky music noise. "Shut the hell up!" I scream. I am angry. Even though I don't know why. "Why are you doing this? Letting everybody push you around. You're just asking for it."

"I'm a rec-rec-rec-record player," Paul says. And spins his hand around in circles.

"Cut it out. You're talking to me now. You don't have to put on a show."

"So?" Paul looks up at me for the first time. "What do you na-na-na-know about anything."

"I know I stopped your skinny ass from getting beat to shit."

"You don't na-know any, anything at all," Paul says. His voice is quavery, though not like he's going to cry. It's more like he really has something he wants to say. "You can, buh-be who you are. I ca-ca-can't do that. You, sh-sh-shitball."

I can't help laughing, which I know immediately is not the right thing to do. Paul comes flying at me, fists swinging in the air, like a broken windmill. I try to wrap him up in my arms, but can't get a hold of him. Some of his punches are landing on my chest and shoulders, but they don't hurt much. "Fucker," Paul yells. "Dirty fucker." He doesn't stutter now.

"It's okay," I say. "I'm sorry, Paul. Really." He is starting to wear down, though still swinging his skinny arms and cursing me out. Then I do manage to grab hold of him and pull him in next to me. "Everything is going to be okay," I tell him again. And let him cry against my chest. "It is, man. It's all going to be okay." Though I know that's not true. Not for Paul and not for me.

First Love

I was glad that my parents let me transfer to John Bartram High School in my sophomore year. It was a lot easier there academically and not so competitive as Central High where everybody was trying to get into Harvard or Yale or at least Penn. Plus Bartram was co-ed – the main attraction. Though I didn't discover girls in any serious way until my junior year. I guess I was slow, and definitely shy. Girls seemed fundamentally different to me. They seemed to know all the things I was still guessing about.

The only girl I spoke to on a regular basis was my older sister, Linda. Speaking is probably the wrong word. What we did was snipe at each other. Linda accused me of anything she thought might get our mother to yell at me. "Butch left all the towels on the bathroom floor," she'd say. "He's such a pig."

"Did not, idiot."

"Mom, did you hear what your little son just said to me?"

"Shut up, pimple face."

"Mom!"

I suspected I might have a better relationship with other girls, but I wasn't sure. Maybe they were all secretly mean or bitchy. Still, I wanted to find out. There was one girl in my English class who I stared at – a lot. Maybe it was because I sat right behind her and so she didn't know (I thought) that I couldn't take my eyes off her. She had long blonde hair that had streaks of brown in it, soft sloping shoulders, and a syrupy voice that I got lost in when she would answer one of Mr. Maimon's questions about Silas Marner or the use of semicolons. It's not that I didn't know how to approach her, it was that I could not even imagine doing such a thing. I was sure that I was not anyone she would ever bother with. I mean, she was seriously pretty and sometimes I'd spot her in the hallways hanging out and laughing with senior guys.

Then one day she turned around and spoke to me. "Did you do the homework, Butch?" I was flabbergasted that she knew my name.

"Yeah, I think so."

"You think so?" She laughed. "You either did it or you didn't."

"Yeah right."

"You're a funny one." She moved to turn back around.

"Do you wanta see it?"

"See what?"

"My homework?"

She laughed. Barbara laughed. And every day after that we talked and shared homework and sometimes walked out of class together, brushing shoulders, the feelings swelling inside me.

It took weeks to get up the nerve. I didn't dare talk to anyone about it. But I wanted to ask Barbara to go out with me. Wanted it in the worst way and was completely petrified by the imagining. I knew if I somehow managed to get the words out and she said no, or worse, didn't take me seriously, I would have to hide under the covers and not get out of bed for the rest of my life.

I fumbled my way through the asking. Barbara helped, laughing and joking and saying, "Sure, I'll go out with you if that's what you're trying to say here."

I was deeply relieved, and then elated. That day we held hands walking out of Mrs. Wendkos' chem class. I asked my dad if I could borrow his old clunker Buick. He didn't say anything, but maybe he was secretly happy that I was going out on a date. He may have even smiled when he tossed me the keys.

Mom was not smiling. "So, who is this girl? What do you know about her?"

I was trying to get out of the house, didn't have time for my mother's interrogation. Was hoping only that I looked okay in my new blue V-neck sweater. "She's just a girl," I said. "No big deal."

Mom lit a cigarette and blew the smoke at the ceiling. "She's Jewish, this girl?"

"No, she's not Jewish. Damn. What's that matter anyway?"

"Don't curse in this house," Mom said.

"Where should I do it?"

"What does that mean?"

"Nothing. Look, I have to leave. I'll see you later."

"When is later?"

"I don't know. Later."

"I want you home by 11 o'clock. Sharp."

"That's ridiculous. It's already 7:30."

"So, you'd better hurry up and go."

"I'm going," I said, deciding not to argue anymore, though I was steaming inside.

"You couldn't go out with a nice Jewish girl?" Mom called after me.

"My parents are insane," I told Barbara. She was settled into the passenger seat.

"All parents are crazy," she said.

I glanced over, stunned that this lovely girl was in my car. She looked even better than she did in class. I couldn't believe my good luck. Then she scooted over close to me on the big bench seat, and my breath caught in my chest. It was all I could do to keep the car on the road.

"I'm glad we're doing this," Barbara said. "I was afraid you'd never ask."

"I was afraid you'd turn me down."

"Why would I do that?"

"Because you're Barbara Davidson."

"What does that mean?"

"It's just that I thought you were sorta out of my league. Really popular, and attractive and all."

Barbara laughed. I liked the sound, soft and tinkly, like bells ringing. "I don't know why people think of me that way. It's not at all how I think of myself. I wasn't even sure if you liked me."

"I like you," I said. "A lot."

She leaned her head against my shoulder. "Where do you wanta go, Butch?"

"Wherever you do."

"I don't care," Barbara said.

"We could just drive then."

"Good."

And so we drove. Mostly just listening to the radio and talking about school, about our parents, and what we wanted to do after high school. It all felt terribly and wonderfully important. Like no other conversation I'd ever had before. I was happy. Sort of a strange feeling.

Two or three hours later I pulled back up in front of Barbara's place. "Come on." She reached over and touched my hand. "Walk me to the door."

I quickly got out and came around to Barbara's side. She took my hand and we walked up the concrete steps toward her front door. Her hand felt soft and warm in mine. I would have been happy to stay in that moment for the rest of my life.

Then we were standing on the top step, in front of the door. "This was really nice, Butch." We were facing each other now, inches apart.

"Yeah, thanks," I said, feeling immediately stupid again.

"You don't have to thank me." Barbara laughed softly.

"I only meant . . ." Then Barbara leaned into me and we kissed.

Though not the first girl I'd ever kissed, it had never been like this before. I felt like Barbara and I had become one person, all warm and delicious and stimulating. Oh my God was I stimulated!

Barbara said, "I have to go in now. My mother will be waiting up."

"Okay,' I said. "I guess I'll see you in school."

"Guess so," Barbara said. "Or you could call me." She smiled and gave me another quick kiss on the lips.

I managed to get back down the stairs and into the car. Started it up and drove off. Before I got to the end of the block, I let out a long whoop, like some kind of crazed cowboy. What a night, I thought. What a goddamned, beautiful night. I looked down at my watch. And I'd even be home by eleven o'clock.

Driving Me Insane

I had been looking forward to turning 16 for at least two years. Because at 16 years of age I'd be able to get my driver's license. And a driver's license signaled entry into the adult world. I had been told that would happen at 13, after my Bar Mitzvah, but that date came and went and I still felt like a kid. I didn't care what the Rabbi said; I hadn't even started to shave.

Now things were different. I still didn't need to shave, but I did have hair on other parts of my body where none had grown before. I even had a girlfriend, who I thought was cute and smart and who had let me put my hand under her blouse, though I mostly just fumbled around and wasn't sure what I was touching. But once I had my own car, well who knew what might happen.

My mother was the one who taught me how to drive. I guess my dad was too busy. I would have been scared anyway to have my dad instruct me, sure that if

I made a mistake he would turn away in disgust. And then where would we be?

Mom was pretty patient with me. I think we both enjoyed doing something together where we didn't have to get angry or embarrassed with each other. And with her wide-bodied, automatic transmission, 1954 Buick Special, it wasn't that hard to learn. We'd practice on back streets where there wasn't much traffic and Mom smoked her Kent cigarettes as I braked carefully at every stop sign. "Good, Butchie," she'd say blowing smoke out the window. "You'll be ready for that test in no time."

"When can I take it? My birthday is tomorrow." I pushed slowly on the accelerator.

"We'll have to ask your father."

"Why? What's he have to do with it?"

"The car is registered to him," Mom said. "He'll have to go with you to the place."

"What place?" I felt my stomach start to knot up.

"The driving place. I don't know. Your father knows where." She flicked her cigarette butt out the open window.

"I don't know about this," I said, shaking my head. I rolled through the next stop sign without even touching the brakes. Luckily no one was coming the other way. Mom didn't even notice.

About a week after my birthday, Dad agreed to accompany me to the Motor Vehicle Department to take my test. "Maybe I could drive on the way over," I said, as we were walking out to the car. I reached my hand out for the keys. "You know, to practice."

"What, are you kidding?" It was like I'd asked him

to take his pants off and do the mambo right there on the sidewalk.

I settled into the passenger seat, feeling a heaviness settle on to my shoulders, a mixture of anger at my dad and fear about the upcoming test. Dad drove the whole way there without saying a word. When I reached out to turn on the radio, he batted my hand away. Maybe it wasn't too great to be 16 after all.

Fortunately, Dad wasn't allowed to stay in the car while I took the test. He stood under the eaves of the Motor Vehicle building smoking a cigar, his face almost invisible underneath his wide-brimmed, brown fedora.

"Your dad seems worried about you," the officer who was administering the test said to me as we pulled away.

"I doubt that," I told him. "He just always looks that way."

The test was easy. I parallel parked correctly, used my turn signals when I was supposed to, and didn't go through any stop signs, even when the officer tried to trick me into doing so. "Just pull over there." He waved his arm, pointing to a spot beyond the last stop sign on the course. But I came to a full stop before proceeding. "Way to do it, kid," the cop said.

They gave me my license right there on the spot and I rushed out of the building to show it to Dad, waving the card around in the air like it was a burning torch.

"So you did it," Dad said. "Mazel Tov."

I was shocked. Did I even see a slight smile crease his face? "So, you want me to drive home now?" I burst out. "With my new license."

"Don't be crazy," Dad said. And held out his open palm. "Give me the damn keys, boy."

You Can't Say That

Every day after high school lets out, I ride the #42 bus home, along with a bunch of other kids. Sometimes we stop and get cigarettes and candy at the drugstore before we get on. Today I buy a pack of Pall Malls and a box of Licorice Nibs. On the bus I sit with my friend Billy Wilson. In the seat in front of us are Charley Kapeghian and Jerry Slice. Charley and I are close, but I don't know Jerry all that well. He's in the commercial track and takes mostly shop classes. Jerry's supposed to be pretty tough. He's wearing a white tee shirt, with the sleeves rolled up so that you can see the muscles in his arms. Charley told me that Jerry Slice even picked fights with the black kids in school, for no reason at all except that he was nuts.

Billy, Charley, and I are *sounding* on each other. It's a sort-of game we play. The worse the insult, the more we laugh. Anything is fair when we're sounding. You can sound on a guy's religion or his ethnic background, on his family, his girlfriend, sound on any damn thing. I take out one of the black Licorice Nibs, hold it up between my fingers and tap Jerry Slice on the shoulder. "Hey," I say, "This looks just like your mother." I am too young and stupid to know how cruel and racist this "joke" is.

Jerry stares at me with a flat expression. Neither Charley or Billy laugh and I know something has gone very wrong. Jerry turns back to the front without saying anything. For the rest of the bus ride, my stomach hurts.

The next day, during 3rd period, Billy Wilson tells me that Jerry is going to "kick your ass."

"How come?" I say.

"You insulted his mother."

"So, big deal. Everybody does that."

"Yeah, but his mother's dead. She died last year from cancer."

"Shit," is all I can say.

"He's coming after you at lunch."

"Shit," I say again.

FOR THE REST OF the morning I feel shaky. Actually, what I feel is scared. I don't want to get in a fight with Jerry Slice. I'm pretty sure he can kick my ass, and, anyway, I don't like to fight. I know that makes me a chicken-shit, but there it is. I haven't had a fight since junior high, and that was pretty much a one-punch affair. Well, make that two. Jack Dyen, the fat fuck, punched me hard in the stomach. Earlier in the day, I had snuck up on him in the cafeteria and stuck a straight pin into the meaty part of his arm. He caught up with me walking home from school. After he hit me, I sank down onto one knee and couldn't move. I'd never felt so taken out of myself as I did then, a mix of surprise, raw pain, and complete humiliation. If this was fighting, I wanted no damn part of it. I caught my breath, got up, and then when fat Jack looked the other way, I punched him in the side of the jaw. It felt almost as good as going down on my knees had felt bad. Jack immediately started crying.

So now Jerry is coming after me and I don't know what to do about it. I think about trying to talk to him and explain that I was only joking around. *Hey, man, no way does a piece of licorice look like your mother. I didn't mean that at all. I was just playing.* I have nothing against Jerry Slice and I don't really see any reason why he should want to beat up on me.

But like I said, Jerry and I are on two different tracks at the high school: I'm in the "block roster", the honors academic group. We all take the same classes and move through the school as a "block." We think we're big deals, the smart kids, the ones who are going to go to college, a lot of us are Jewish. And Jerry Slice is in the commercial track, for kids who are going to be plumbers and carpenters and not go to college. The dummies, is how we think of them. So I'll never be able to talk to Jerry before lunchtime, when he will already be looking to get me. I just have to play it cool for the rest of the day. Not let anybody see that I'm scared. That's not something you want your buddies, to know.

At lunchtime, my friends and I leave the building to buy sandwiches at Dom's, a hoagie shop. It's about a two-block walk from the school building and halfway between Dom's and the school, Jerry Slice catches up with me.

"Hey," I hear, a second before he grabs me by the shoulder and pulls me around. Here I am, facing him. With everybody else circled around us, like boys do when there's gonna be a fight. The first thing I do is shit my pants. I'm not lying. A hard little turd shoots straight out of my butt into my underpants. I pray nobody will notice.

"Hey, man," I say, trying to keep the shake out of my voice, "How you doin'?"

"Who do you think you are?" Jerry says, scrunching up his jaw.

"I don't know," I say. "Nobody special." I take a step back. Jerry's an inch or two shorter than I am, but his shoulders are wider and his neck is thick like a football player. He's got a black smudge across his cheek, looks like grease.

"What you said about my mother, take it the fuck back." His fists are balled up.

"Sure, I'll take it back," I say. And add, "I – I didn't even know your mother."

"How would you?" Jerry says.

"I wouldn't. I'm sure she was a good lady."

"Fucking A," Jerry says. There's a catch in his voice.

"I'm really sorry, man." I don't feel like a chicken shit saying this. I do feel sorry for Jerry now. He's probably a decent kid. "I don't know what I'd do if I lost my mom. And I don't even like her very much."

Jerry laughs. "Yeah, I know what you mean." Then he jumps bad again. "I should still kick your ass." He steps toward me.

"I said I was sorry, man." I shrug. "What else you want me to do?" I notice that I'm not scared anymore. It's gone beyond that somehow. If Jerry Slice wants to punch me in the face, I don't even care.

"You got a token?" Jerry says.

"A token?"

"Yeah, man, a token. For the bus. I don't have any to get home." Jerry steps back, lets his hands dangle at his sides.

I reach in my pocket to make sure the smooth metal tokens are there. I buy a package of them every week. It's cheaper than paying the bus fare each time. "Sure, man, I can lend you a token." I pull it out and hold it in my hand.

"Awright," Jerry says. "I can pay you back later."

"Don't worry about it. No big deal." I hand him the token and he takes it.

"I said I'd pay you back."

"Fine," I say.

The circle around us begins to fall back, the boys losing interest, disappointed that likely nobody's going to get punched out.

"So, forget about that thing I said before?" I hold out my hand to shake. Jerry waits a moment and tries to do a stare-down, but I don't back away, and finally he puts his hand out and we shake. The whole group then moves on to the hoagie shop, like nothing ever happened and we all just better grab our sandwiches quick before the bell rings. I know I have to get to a stall in the boy's room.

I CAN'T SAY THAT Jerry Slice and I became best friends after that. I'd nod to him if I ever saw him around school, but that was about it. I still thought it was best to keep my distance. Jerry went into the Army after Bartram High. I went on to college, later grad school, and had student deferments. Somebody told me that Jerry Slice got sent to Vietnam. Who knows where he is now, or even if he's alive. He's never come to any class reunions. We had our fiftieth last year. I asked Billy Wilson then if he remembered that day Jerry and I almost fought. "Doesn't ring a bell," Billy said.

"Yeah, no big deal," I said. I was surprised at how old Billy looked. He probably was thinking the same about me.

"I just hope he had a good life," I said, but Billy had already turned away.

I'm Going to Be a Writer

It is 1962. This is the year I discover "literature." I've always read a lot, but they have mostly been books about sports or inspirational biographies, or those condensed Reader's Digest books my parents get in the mail. Now I find that books can be much more than this, that they take me away from all my worries, lift me up, make me happy, even sometime make me cry – though I don't tell anyone else about this.

My sister Linda is in college, at the University of Pennsylvania, though she still lives at home. She brings books from her lit class home and places them on the wooden bookshelf in her bedroom – a place I have been expressly forbidden from entering. Which only makes me go in there more frequently. I read all the novels that appear on that little shelf: *Madame Bovary* (very sexy), *The Hunchback of Notre Dame* (which I at first mistake for another sports book), Gatsby, *The Sun Also Rises*, which I think is the most romantic book I've ever read till Linda tells me that Hemingway hates Jews. I even try *The Sound and The Fury*, but have no idea what is going on. Then it shows up. A slim paperback titled *The Catcher In The Rye*. It's about this kid Holden Caulfield who thinks everybody except his little sister, Phoebe, is a big phony. I feel like Holden and I are the same person – so much so that I can hardly stand to finish the book. And now all I want to do is be a writer and write books like J.D. Salinger.

The problem is I don't know how to actually write something. They don't teach us that in school. In my high school English class we read Silas Marner and diagram sentences. Still I decide to try, and begin scribbling stories in my school notebooks. I do it all the time, even during class. After dinner, which in our house are silent affairs, I rush up to my 3rd floor bedroom and pull the notebook from under my mattress. I don't want my mother to discover it, or any of them to know what I am doing. For some reason, writing stories feels sort of shameful, somehow associated with my blossoming (exploding) sexuality. Maybe the connection is not so mysterious. I have also discovered *Playboy Magazine*. I read it at the newsstand near my house, until the owner starts giving me dirty looks. He thinks I'm looking at the pictures of the naked women, which I am – intently, ravenously; but I am also reading the stories in the magazine. They are pretty amazing also. And not even always sexy. I feel completely transported by these short stories, often written by some of the best writers in the country, Ray Bradbury, Joseph

Heller, even Norman Mailer. I decide right then to be a short story writer. And to be published in *Playboy*.

Pretty soon I have finished my first short story. It's about a troubled boy who stares in the window of his next-door neighbor's house because he thinks he's in love with their daughter, even though the boy has never spoken to the girl. Then one night he sees the girl walk by an open window and she is completely naked, which makes him feel both guilty and sad.

I think it is a pretty good story, but really have no way of knowing and nobody to show it to, who might give me some feedback. Actually, I can't even imagine sharing my writing with anybody. I would be way too embarrassed for that. What I do instead is type the story up, put it in an 8x10 manila envelope and mail it to the fiction editor at *Playboy Magazine* in Chicago. I don't then realize what chutzpah, what foolishness, it takes for a 16 year old kid to send his first attempt at fiction writing to a national magazine, but that's what I do.

A few weeks later, the response arrives. Unfortunately, my mother intercepts the envelope before I get home from school. And, of course, despite it being clearly addressed to me, she has opened it. When I arrive home and head to my bedroom sanctuary, Mom is waiting for me, manila envelope in hand, which I can clearly see has been ripped open. "You want to tell me what this is?" she asks, as if she doesn't know.

"It's my story, I guess." I reach for the envelope. Despite the current circumstances, I am still desperate to know what the editors have had to say. But Mom pulls it away. "This is filthy! Where do you get such ideas?"

"I make them up."

"Well, it's disgusting. And not even a good story." She throws the brown envelope down on the bed and turns to leave. "Don't think I won't tell your father about this."

"Tell him. I don't care," I shout.

"Disgusting," she says again as she leaves the room. I'm pretty sure she won't tell my father about the story. She's more afraid of getting him upset than I am.

As soon as she is gone, I grab the envelope and pull the typed pages out. There is a note attached. My heart is pounding now, and not just because of what has happened with my mother. I take a deep breath and read:

> Dear Mr. Freedman,
>
> Thank you for submitting your story, "The Girl Next Door" to *Playboy Magazine*. Our editors have read your work very carefully, and though it does not meet our needs at this time, we would encourage you to continue to pursue your writing goals and to submit future efforts to the magazine.
>
> Thank you.

I let out a long sigh, realize I haven't breathed since opening the letter, and then, then I jump up off the bed and yell. "It's good, damn it. They fucking liked it!"

Of course, the letter said no such thing. And, as I later realized, it was no more than a form letter, the same sent probably to thousands of unsuccessful writers. But that didn't matter. What mattered was that the letter meant (to me anyway) that I was now a writer. Goddamn right I'd be sending future efforts to their magazine, and to a lot of other places also. I didn't care what my mother thought or said, I was going to keep writing. It's what I had to do.

Saving Lives – Including My Own

This is the best job ever. I get to sit on the beach all day long, talk to girls, listen to the radio, go swimming, and get paid for it. Oh yeah, and if someone starts to drown I'm supposed to save them. I had to pass a test before they would hire me. Along with a bunch of other guys, I had to swim out into the ocean for about half a mile to where there was a buoy bouncing around, then turn around and swim back as fast as possible. Only the best swimmers would be considered. I was the first one back. I sorta caught a wave on the way in. So they hired me – just like that. And now here I am, sitting up on top of this high white chair, my whistle around my neck, zinc oxide on my nose, sunglasses in place. Feeling good. There are a few kids playing in the water, but they're staying pretty close to shore, so I take the time to scan the beach for hot girls. So far, nothing much, but the day is young. I turn on my portable radio, lean back, and close my eyes. Got to get more sleep, is the last thing I remember thinking till the damn kids started yelling.

"Help, help, help! My sister's drowning." A little boy in a bathing suit is shouting up at me from beneath the chair, and for a moment I have no idea where I am, then I jump up – and almost fall off the chair. And the next thing I know I've hopped down and am running full blast into the surf. It's all instinct and fear now. I plunge into the ocean and start madly swimming toward where a bunch of people are now pointing and somehow, as if guided by something other than my own mind, I latch onto the skinny arm of the drowning little girl, and pull her to me. She's still alive, thank God, and I walk out of the surf carrying her in my arms. People are actually cheering for me as I lay the child on the sand. She coughs once, then smiles up at me.

I feel sort of guilty, even though my boss, Lieutenant Louie, told me after the rescue, "You're doing a great job, kid." So now, I make sure I stay awake all the time and watch the water like a mother watches her baby. Even when I'm talking to girls, I keep one eye on the waves. I've had to make a couple more saves as the summer has gone on – seven all together. Each one scared me more than the last. It's not something you get used to. Sometimes I think this isn't the right job for me. It's too much responsibility for a kid like me. But I can't quit now. What would be my excuse? And, anyway, I need the money. Not just for the summer expenses, but also I'm supposed to be saving up for college, which seems a little bit weird and distant to me.

I don't even really know if I want to go to college. It's just one of those things – at least in our family – that everybody assumes is going to happen. An expectation I guess you'd call it.

I've been thinking lately that what I'd really like to do is become a full-time surfer. Follow the waves, you know. Maybe go to California or Hawaii and take part-time jobs and spend the rest of the time chasing waves. I hear they've got some crazy swells on the Big Island. Of course, this fantasy is not something I could share with my parents. Once they stopped laughing, they would tell me to "get serious, boy." But I'm tired of having to be serious, and tired of doing what's expected of me. I'm starting to feel like maybe there's a bigger world out there than I ever expected. It's a lot like lifeguarding. You start out thinking it's gonna be one way and then you discover the job (or your life) is really not like that at all.

Now it's Labor Day weekend – a very crowded beach day, and the last week lifeguards will be on duty. As I look around, I see hundreds of people. Older folks sitting in beach chairs, with umbrellas poked in the sand to keep the sun off; groups of teenagers spread out on blankets, transistor radios blaring out rock and roll; and lots of younger kids running all over the place – their parents not even trying to keep an eye on them. I guess they figure that's what I'm there for. But I'm trying to watch every inch of the surf, which is just about broiling with kids and rafts, swimmers and paddlers, all jumping over the waves, which are breaking pretty hard today. I watch one young kid, maybe twelve years old, dive under a big breaker and wait for him to come up on the other side, which thankfully he does. Then I'm blowing my whistle and waving at a couple other people who have drifted away from the flags that mark the safe area. At first they ignore me, so I jump off the stand, land with a thud on the sand, and walk briskly down toward the surf and blast them again with the whistle. Now they wave and start to move back where they belong. This little bit of authority feels good to me.

I manage to get through the whole day with nobody drowning, and no emergencies other than using my first aid kit to put band aids on a few cuts and scrapes and mend one bloody nose on a kid who was body surfing and plowed into some fat guy's backside. It could have been worse. They both ended up laughing.

Now it's six o'clock and everyone has left the beach. My shift is over and I feel tired, but happy. It was cool being a lifeguard, and I think, overall, I did a good job. For the first time in my life, I'm beginning to get outside of myself, if you know what I mean. This job was all about keeping other people safe. I almost never even thought about myself. There just wasn't time for that. And I'm starting to think that's maybe a good thing, and maybe something I can try to remember and use in the next few months and years when I'm trying to figure out what the hell to do with my life.

As I pull the lifeguard stand back beyond the high tide line, a few seagulls swoop down toward me, so close I can feel the wind from their wings beating around my head. It startles me. Are these damn birds attacking me? The gulls, big ugly grey ones, circle around and come toward me again. It's like they've been waiting for this, my last day, to come and get me. Like in "The Birds", that Hitchcock movie I saw. Now I move quickly to get the stand where it belongs and get the hell off the beach. It is definitely time to be moving on.

Leaving on the Greyhound

It's September and I'm leaving to go off for my first year in college.

My father drives me and my friend, Bobby Fisher, who is going to the same school, to the Greyhound bus station in downtown Philadelphia. Mom stays at home. She's still angry about my decision to go to this unworthy little out-of-town school. Dad, however, is acting unusually friendly. It is so unlike him. At home, we rarely speak – I mean, ever. And all through high school he has ignored me. Never even came to my basketball games. In the car he asks Fisher about his college plans, and seems genuinely interested when Bobby says he is going to concentrate on math and physics.

At the bus station Dad buys my ticket for me – one way to Marietta, Ohio. I've never even visited this school, Marietta College, picked it at random from a shelf full of college catalogs in the school counselor's office. Anything to avoid going to the University of Pennsylvania, where Dad is an alumnus, and having to stay at home.

"So, do you have everything you need?" Dad asks. He's wearing a dark suit and a bowtie, like he always does, and an overcoat and hat, even though it's officially still summer.

"Yeah, I guess so." I have no idea what I need for college. I filled up my suitcase last night with the clothes I already own. And I threw in my transistor radio, the one I use to listen to WDAS, the soul station, when everyone else has gone to sleep.

"How about money?" Dad asks.

"You've already given me money."

"So, maybe you need some more. Maybe you'll want to go out for dinner."

"I signed up for the cafeteria meals Dad. They feed you breakfast lunch and dinner."

"Still, maybe you'll want a snack." He pulls a twenty-dollar bill from his wallet. "Maybe you'll go on a date even." Dad smiles at me.

I don't know what to make of him. This guy who has always been so damn gloomy. Now he's acting like my best friend. "Okay, thanks." I put the money in my back pocket.

Fisher nudges my arm. "Hey, man, the bus is here."

Dad picks up my suitcase and starts toward the loading area, walking quickly.

"I can carry that," I shout after him. "It's heavy."

"Don't worry, Butchy," he yells back over his shoulder. "It's my pleasure."

Such a strange thing for him to say. I look over at Fisher. He's struggling with his own two suitcases, but meets my look and I raise my eyebrows and nod at my father, like he's some kind of crazy person. Fisher just shrugs his shoulders. He must have other things on his mind.

Dad scurries on ahead and hands off my leather suitcase to the bus driver, who is busily loading bags into the cargo hold under the bus. "My boy is going off to college," Dad tells the driver, who only nods and keeps working, "It's his first year. He's a freshman."

"He doesn't care, Dad. Can't you see that?"

"Maybe he does." Dad looks contrite, but recovers quickly and holds out his hand. And we shake. Dad holds on, then pulls me in for a hug. I don't think my dad and I have ever hugged before. "I'll miss you, son," he says.

"Yeah, sure." I pull my hand away. "Me too, I guess."

FISHER AND I BOARD the bus and find an open double seat all the way in the back. I sit by the window. As the bus starts to back out of its slip, I see Dad come running back alongside the slowly moving bus. Now he's waving and grinning, practically sprinting to keep up with the reversing bus. I don't remember ever having seen him run before. I feel embarrassed. I turn to Fisher, point at my dad, and say, "What an asshole."

Fisher laughs.

When I look out the window again, Dad has stopped running – and smiling. He gazes down at the ground, then turns to leave, and doesn't look back.

I know he has read my lips. I think about trying to get off the bus and run after him. But it's too late now. We're almost out in the street. I feel sick to my stomach. But I'm too young and smug and fucking self-centered to realize what I've just done. It doesn't pay to think about such things. I mean just because he's nice to me one time doesn't mean I'm going to forget all the rest of it. "What the hell, huh?" I say to Fisher. "We're going to college, man."

"Yeah," he says. "Cool." Then he pulls out a paperback and starts reading.

I laugh for no reason, then I decide to put what happened with my father out of my head. He's probably already forgotten it, I tell myself. But somewhere I know that's not true. Not even a little bit.

Part Three

Running with Blinders

Jew Bunny – Part 2

There was a Jewish fraternity at the small liberal arts college that I attended. But I was ideologically opposed to any of the Greek societies that dominated the campus social life. Or maybe I just avoided them for fear that they would reject me. By this time I was a bit of a recluse, definitely an outsider. I was not happy with myself, nor with the environment I found myself in – a college out in the middle of nowhere (Ohio) with a bunch of other students who I believed I had nothing in common with and so did very little to make friends. Coming from a big city, and from a diverse ethnic environment, I was put off by the unrelenting sameness (the paleness) of the kids around me. Perhaps, I would have found common cause with the guys in that Jewish fraternity. But instead of rushing their house, I stayed as far away from them as possible. In truth, I felt repulsed. A bunch of ugly, obnoxious, rich Jews, I decided, most of them from New York City or Long

Island. I knew all the rest of the fraternities loved to beat up on them in the intramural sports leagues. Jews, of course, were lousy at sports. Everybody knew that. (I believed it too, despite the fact that I had played with lots of super-athletic Jewish ball players back in Philly and idolized Sandy Koufax. Talk about confusion.) So, no way was I going near those guys.

None of this was new territory. For thousands of years one popular survival technique for Jews was to assimilate, to try to blend in with the dominant culture and reject their (hideous) Jewishness. This was, I learned, the case in Eastern Europe and Germany before Hitler changed everyone's reality, or maybe opened their eyes to the true reality. Hitler didn't make fine distinctions about who was a Jew and who wasn't.

What was I? A self-hating Jew. But one without even that self-knowledge, and no way to get it, except to keep stumbling along in denial. The next step? You guessed it. I decided to marry out of the religion.

I thought my parents would be pleased when I broke the news that I was engaged to Catherine Rolling. Mom and Dad had just arrived on campus for my graduation (their first visit in the four years I'd been there) and I was anxious to introduce them to my intended. I thought she was perfect; blonde hair, blue eyes, cute little pug nose. She was even a member of one of the snootier sororities; one which I'm certain did not accept Jews. What she wanted with me, I had no idea. Certainly I wasn't a prize catch. She could easily, I thought, have had any of the good-looking, clean-cut fraternity boys. I hadn't even hidden the fact that I was Jewish from her. Little did I know then, that my 'foreignness' was why she had chosen me. But that's another long and twisted tale. For now, all I cared about was showing her off to my parents. Wouldn't Mom be thrilled. No mouthy, big-nosed Jewish girls for her boy.

"Rolling?" my mother said. "That doesn't sound like a Jewish name."

"It's not." My Dad said.

"I never said it was," I said.

"So, what's going on here?" Mom wanted to know. "You're marrying this girl?"

"Yes. I thought you'd be pleased."

"Pleased?" Mom always turned everything into a question. "Why would we be pleased?"

"Because she's pretty and nice. And not even Jewish."

"This is what you think we want?" Mom's mouth hung open. "That you should marry a non-Jew, a blondie shiksa?"

"Yeah, I guess I did." This was not going the way I thought it would.

"Do you hear what the boy is telling us, Meyer?" She turned her sour face to my father.

"I hear," he said, but didn't look at me.

"Well, I don't give a shit what you think," I yelled. Once again I had severely misjudged my parents' wants and needs, and also apparently completely misunderstood the implied messages of my upbringing about what it meant to be Jewish.

Of course, they didn't want me to marry a gentile girl. Over the years to come they made it more and more clear that they didn't think Cathy was either bright enough or accomplished enough to marry into the family. And even if my wife had been a brilliant scientist or a concert pianist (she was neither) she still would have been rejected for one very simple reason: her non-Jewish blood would water down and diminish the future generations of our family, or specifically, my future children. With a gentile mother, my children would not be considered Jewish, even if Cathy were to convert, which she had no intention of doing and, which I never asked her to do. I thought it was all ridiculous, if I even thought about it at all. But maybe there was some validity to the whole strange intermarriage rejection. I don't think my mother could have articulated her position; it was something deeper than logic with her, something that allowed her to hold her own self-hating, anti-Semitic views, while at the same time embodying the tribal needs of an entire race of people. A necessity, some would say, if Jews were to remain a viable culture. Intermarriage, particularly in America, was seriously diluting the stock. Apparently, there were many young men like myself, who only wanted to marry shiksas. We had been taught well, but little did our parents realize what the results would be, a diminishment of the whole culture, both in numbers and belief.

If I could imagine a different reality, a different history, one where I was raised to appreciate my culture and religion, and to be proud of our people, maybe this would have happened instead: I would have spent more time (or most of the time) with other Jews, and when it came time to marry (after my trip to Israel and time living on a kibbutz), I would have married a Jewish woman, with dark curly hair, brown eyes, and strong opinions she wasn't afraid of expressing. And we would have raised our children to appreciate who they were and the long history and struggles of our people. It's a regret. But not one that I can reasonably blame myself for. The environment I was raised in was not conducive to either strength or self-knowledge. Not for my parents and not for me. I see now a whole generation of Jewish men and women of my generation and later generations, who don't know who they are, and worse, don't care. In rejecting the Jewish religion as archaic or unnecessary or uncool, they likewise reject all the pain and suffering, the joy and accomplishments, the fucking epic survival ability of all our forebears. And I'm afraid that this is a downward spiral, at least in the U.S., that eventually leads to complete assimilation and loss of identity.

Maybe being Jewish is beyond articulation. Maybe that's what my parents thought that I would understand without them having to explain it. You're a Jew because you're a Jew. And that's all there is to it. Now follow the rules, boy.

But I'm afraid my parents were misguided in their assumptions. They were wrong not to explain to my siblings and me exactly what it did mean to be Jewish. And when we were old enough (10-12?) certainly we should have heard the painful story of our European relatives and other Jews who had perished in the holocaust and why they thought that happened, and what became of the survivors, and how about Israel? Tell me something, anything, please. So my first experience of learning about the concentration camps doesn't come in a high school social studies classroom watching a grainy 16mm film showing piles of human bodies bulldozed into ditches, Jewish bodies, skeletal, frightening, beyond belief. What does a young person do in the absence of coherency, the absence of information about who one is? Some of my classmates giggled during the showing.

I refused to think about what I saw in that newsreel film. I didn't ask my parents about it or my grandparents or anyone else. I buried it in my subconscious, deep down, alongside all the other barely understood, barely mentioned information about personal identity, all of which added up to a raging sense of inadequacy, shame, and anger. All of which drove me away from Judaism for the next 30 years. My time in the desert, perhaps.

Are You Sure about This, Kid?

I've only just graduated from college and don't really know what to do next so I stumble on to the next dumb thing. I didn't know it, but I was looking for a life ring, something to hang on to. No, maybe I did know it, just couldn't admit it.

"You can marry her if you have to, but don't expect me to come to the wedding." My mother lit a cigarette then to emphasize her seriousness, or maybe just because it was time for her next cigarette. She blew the smoke in my direction.

"What about Dad?" I asked.

"What about him?"

"Does he feel the same way?"

"You think your father is going to go into a church? To watch you marry your shiksa?"

"I don't know. He's never said anything to me about it. I'd like to know what he thinks."

"I'll tell you what he thinks," Mom said. "That's all you have to know."

There was nowhere else to go with the argument. And strangely I wasn't feeling particularly upset. I'd already used up all my anger in the previous weeks and years. Mom and I were locked into position. Nothing I could do, short of becoming a doctor like my father, would ever satisfy her. And since I had a serious aversion to the sight of blood, it was clear to me that Mom and I were never going to be best buddies.

Still, there was something I needed to know. I didn't really care if my parents came to my wedding or not. Truthfully, I wasn't sure *I* wanted to be there. And, if even more honesty is called for (as it always is) I'd have to admit that I didn't want to marry this girl at all. Hardly knew her. Or she, me. We were two dumb kids flailing about, trying to make sense of a post-college world and each eager, for our own twisted reasons, to flaunt our parents' deepest desires: that we stay with our own kind.

As a last grasp at coherence, I arranged to speak to my father. I say arranged, because speaking to my dad was not an event that occurred naturally. I doubt we had had three real conversations the entire time I had grown up in his house. And two of those were about the Philadelphia Phillies. Most of the time I felt he was angry with me or disappointed, or simply disinterested.

What I mostly knew about him, perhaps the only thing, was his silence. It was as if he lived inside a bubble of his own construction. I could see in, but I couldn't reach in and touch. Mom was the protector of the bubble. "Don't bother your father," she'd constantly tell my brother and me. "He's a very busy man." Or if something went awry at school or in the neighborhood, she'd proclaim, "If Dad heard that he'd be furious." But Dad was rarely furious, or even upset. Certainly he was reserved, contained, maybe thoughtful. And sometimes, watch out kid, he did explode in rage. But how was I to know what was really going on in there.

Dad told me to come down to his office after dinner. His office took up the first floor of our three-story house. Every evening from 5:30 to 8:30 Dad had office hours, the waiting room filled with sad faced patients, each eager to see Doctor Freedman. He was an important man in our working class, West Philadelphia neighborhood. That was one thing I did know about my dad.

Now I sat opposite him, like one of his patients. Dad behind his big oak desk. He pushed aside a stack of medical journals and stared across at me. He wasn't smiling, but he wasn't frowning either. I took this as a very good sign.

"So?" he said, and leaned back in his chair. "What's on your mind, son?"

My power of speech evaporated. Had he just called me 'son'? Dad had rarely, if ever, even called me by my first name. If he had occasion to address me at all, it was 'boy'. As I struggled to form the words I had carefully rehearsed earlier, Dad seemed content to wait.

"Well, Dad," I began, choking out the words, nervous in this new territory. "It's about this getting married deal."

He nodded and sat back up. "Your mother told me. I think your mom's a bit upset."

"She always is." I scooched my chair closer to the desk. "I don't think she likes my girlfriend very much."

"She doesn't know her very well yet. We've only met her the one time at your graduation, son."

He said "son" again. What the hell was going on here? Was this man really my father?

"That's what I told her," I said. "I told Mom she should get to know Cathy better before she makes all these judgments."

"What did she say to that?"

"She said, 'I know all I need to know'."

I thought I saw the whisper of a smile. "Yes, well, your mother has strong opinions." He reached for his pipe and tobacco.

"But do you think it's okay then?" I persisted.

"What's that?" He packed a pinch of tobacco into the pipe and tamped it down. The musky aroma wafted over, like sweetly rotting fruit.

"Getting married," I said. "To Cathy. In a church."

"Those are three different issues," Dad said.

"Right." I was feeling somewhat adrift.

"The more important question," Dad said, stopping to light a match and take a few beginning puffs, "is do *you* want to get married?"

"Well, yeah," I said. "Sort of."

"Why?" Now he was definitely smiling.

"Why?" I repeated, dumbfounded. I had not prepared for this question. I hadn't even really discussed it with my intended. I shrugged my shoulders. "I think it's the right time now." I knew that sounded weak, so I added. "And I really do like her."

"I've heard worse reasons," Dad said. "What are you going to do for money?"

"I'm thinking about taking a teaching job." I swallowed hard. This was the first I'd told him or my mother about this new direction. I was sure Dad would be crushed by the news that Med school was now completely out of the question, as my mother had led me to believe he would be.

"Wonderful," Dad said. "I've often thought that teaching would be a good field for you."

"You have?"

"Absolutely. You're a very caring person. And smart too. What else do you need to be a good teacher?"

I'm sure my mouth was hanging open now, but I pushed on. "So, you think it's okay to go ahead and get married?"

"I can't make that decision for you, son."

I smiled. I was getting used to being a son. "And you'll come to the wedding?"

Dad put his pipe down in the heavy cut glass ashtray on his desk. "No. Your mother's right about that. Seeing you married in a church would break our hearts. I'm sorry."

"That's okay," I said quickly, sensing that this might be my way out. "Maybe we'll elope."

"That might not be a bad idea," he said. Dad stood then and reached his hand across the desk. What the hell was this? What did he want? Then it dawned on me. I stood up, and met his hand. We shook, firmly, warmly, and we looked in each other's eyes. "I've got patients waiting," he said after a few seconds, and dropped his gaze.

"Right," I said, and moved to open the office door.

"We can talk again," Dad said before I was out the door.

I turned back. "I'd like that," I said. "I really would."

So You Want to Be a Teacher

There wasn't much to do with a degree in English when I graduated from Marietta College. I wanted to be a writer, but I couldn't tell anybody that. Hardly admitted it to myself. Still I had to find a job and make some money, so I managed to finagle a position with the Philadelphia School district. My dad helped, which felt a bit weird. He was the medical superintendent for the district and so had some pull. I never even thanked him. That's the kind of guy I was then.

I got a job at West Philadelphia High, an all-black school in a tough neighborhood. But the teaching does not go well. I'm trying hard to relate, to do the right thing, but feeling frustrated and inept. It takes so much energy to go into that classroom every morning and try and teach students who, from everything I can tell, have little or no interest in anything I have to say.

It isn't like an open rebellion, nobody's threatening me or throwing books around. It isn't "Blackboard Jungle" or "Up The Down Staircase." Those movies have it all wrong. These kids are just passing time, waiting till they're old enough to graduate or drop out. They already know that all the odds are stacked against them and the most they can hope for is a minimum wage job and even for that they'll need to claim a high school education. So they sit here, passing the day, letting me natter on.

I ask the other teachers, the ones who've been around for some time, how they handle things. "How do you get them inspired? How do you even get them to answer questions?"

"Give them tests," Larry Parkman tells me. "That passes the time and keeps them busy." Parkman teaches social studies and has been at West Philly High for over twenty years. He's "seen it all change," he tells me. He sits back and lights up yet another cigarette. The teacher's lounge is always thick with cigarette smoke. I don't think there's anyone who doesn't smoke, not even the phys ed people.

"But they won't study for a test. Most of them don't even remember to bring their textbooks to class."

"Doesn't matter. It's just busy work. You're gonna pass them all anyway." Larry leans back in the green vinyl chair and props his feet up on the low table that separates us. He's wearing puffy, orthopedic shoes.

"Why would I do that? I suspect half of my kids don't even know how to read."

Parkman smirks. "So, what's that tell you?"

"That someone's been dropping the ball big time for a lot of years?"

"No, rookie. It tells you that we believe in *social promotion*." He makes bunny ears in the air around the words.

"Social promotion? I'm almost afraid to ask what that means." I look at my watch and feel a pang in my stomach. Third period's coming up and I don't know what I'm gonna do with them. Senior English.

"It means that we're all in this together, kid. We pass them on to the next grade and the next and eventually out into the world with a minimum of hassle and in return the students spend their time here without causing any major damage. Maybe they even learn something. Everybody wins." Parkman swings his feet off the table and sits up. "You'll figure it out before long."

"I don't know. That sounds awfully cynical." I don't want to tell him what I really think. I still have to get along with guys like this.

"The world's a cynical place, buddy boy. Maybe they forgot to tell you that in college."

Well, fuck you. Maybe I will say what I think. "Shit, how do you live with yourself? What's the point?"

Parkman's brow knits together, his tired eyes come to life. For a second I think he's gonna jump across the table and throttle me. Part of me is hoping he will try. "Look, asshole, you come talk to me after you've been here twenty years. Then we'll talk about the point. All I know is that when I go home at the end of the day to my wife and kids, I can look at myself in the mirror and know I'm taking care of business."

"What business is that?" I lean down to pick up my books and papers. I want to get out of here.

"Education, kid. Edu-fuckin-cation." Then he laughs.

On the way out of the workroom I stop by the water cooler and pop another diet pill. That's what my mother calls them. The name on the bottle of pills that I "found" in my father's office was dexamphetamine. I've been taking them now every day for the past couple weeks. I feel like they make me a better teacher, or at least one who has something to say. I drink a lot of coffee too. A lot. The last time I weighed myself I was down to 160. In college, I weighed 185. I just want to make it to winter break. Then I'll have a couple weeks off and can get my head back together.

"Okay, everyone take out a piece of paper and a pencil," I announce to the class. "We're going to have a spelling test."

A couple kids reach into their notebooks and remove pieces of lined paper. I can hear the snap of the clasps on their 3-ring binders. But most of them continue to look down at the desks in front of them.

"Raise your hand if you need paper," I say. Then walk around the room distributing sheets of paper to most of the students. I repeat the same process with pencils. "Now write your name and today's date at the top of the sheet. It's December 10th." Everybody does what I say without complaint. That feels promising. The dexxie is also starting to kick in and I feel a thrumming in my gut and a need to explain myself to the class. "Spelling is very important. Well, maybe not very important. It's actually kind of arbitrary when you really think about it. I mean there could be a hundred different ways to spell the same word. Think about a word like milk. I mean why not spell it m-e-l-k or m-e-e-l-k or even m-y-l-k."

"You saying milk is the first word on the test?" Arthur Bundy asks. Arthur sits in the front row all alone.

"No, that was only an example of the vagaries of English spelling."

"So, how do you spell it?" Arthur asks. He wears thick glasses and is one of the kids who actually tries.

"Spell what?"

"Milk, man. Is it with a E or a Y?"

"Well, neither actually, Arthur." Arthur shakes his head and looks away. "The point is that no matter how difficult spellings can sometimes be, we still need to learn how to do it. You'll find when you get out into the world that people judge you on all sorts of extraneous things, things that really have nothing to do with what sort of person you are or what your native intelligence might be. You may find it hard to believe, but the same thing happens to me all the time. People decide that I'm such and such a way because that's what I look like or speak like, when really I'm a whole different sort of person. I find that's true with even the people I'm closest with in the whole world." I pause to catch my breath and look out at the room, the students now staring at me with what I take to be interest. "The thing is, you have to be able to spell. Even if it doesn't mean diddley squat." My mood suddenly swings into despair. What the hell am I doing? Who really cares about any of this shit? We're all losers here. That's what I should be telling them. Give it up, kids. There ain't nothing out there for you but a long, awful trip to the grave.

"Mister Freedman." The voice from the back of the room brings me out of my funk. "You gonna give us the test or what?"

"Yeah, right, the test." I gather myself, blink my eyes a few times then look at the piece of paper in front of me with the words I have decided to test them on. They come from a list of commonly misspelled words that I found in the English Department's workroom. "First word is misspell." I smile. "See that, you can even misspell, misspell."

Most of them write something down on their papers, but nobody laughs.

"Number two is the word, believe. Remember the rule and you won't go wrong." I'm sort of having fun now and teaching them some good lessons at the same time.

"Don't know no rules," one of the boys who sits in the last row grumbles. I squint to see who it is and see Thomas Jefferson. I always get a kick out of saying his whole name, and then saying, "My man, the father of the constitution."

"Sure you do," I say. "You've probably heard it every year that you've been in school. 'I before E except after C'."

"What's that mean?" Thomas says. "Why you always talking in riddles?"

I think I might show an example on the chalkboard, but that would take too much time. "Let's go on to word number three. Conscience. A way to remember this word is to pronounce it con-science. Like Con with Science." Again, the class stares at me with equal parts confusion and disinterest. It's no use. All my good tips are for nothing with these kids. They don't care, don't want to learn. Maybe Parkman is right. Just do your time and move on. "The next word is foreign," I announce. "I'm not even going to bother to tell you the trick to it."

"Good," Arthur Bundy mutters.

I hope I can make it to the end of the day, is what I'm thinking. I sit back down behind my desk and search around in my pockets for another greenie. There are still four periods to go.

To Mexico – by Way of West Virginia

It was summer and it was hot and humid, like summers are in Philadelphia. My wife and I were living in our first apartment, a fourth-floor walk-up that overlooked the football field of the high school where I taught English during the school year. Some of my students had discovered that by climbing up to the top row of the bleacher seats they could peer into the windows of our apartment. I wanted to get out of town. Way out.

"Let's go to Mexico," I said.

"What'd you say?" Cathy was doing something or other in the kitchen and the bulky air conditioner rattled away in the window.

I walked over to where she stood and held up the book I had been reading. "*Mexico on Five Dollars a Day.* I want to go there. We could drive."

She continued to wash the dishes in the sink. "Isn't that a very long drive?

"Uh huh."

"Can we go through West Virginia on the way?" She looked up at me for the first time.

"Sure. Why not."

"Okay then." She smiled. "Let's do it." I think I must have felt tender toward her then, but I didn't show it. Instead I went back to the couch and thought about how exactly to get us to Mexico. I had a fairly new VW Beetle with a sunroof and a zippy little engine and I loved driving it. We can do this, I thought. And so we packed up and left.

We followed main roads, highlighted on the map I'd gotten from Triple A, then made a detour into the backwoods of West Virginia where Cathy's grandparents lived on a farm surrounded by other farms. When we got off the interstate and on to those little country roads, C said she wanted to drive. "This is my home, Butch," she said.

"Yeah, but it's my car." I pulled over, though, and we switched seats. Her driving seemed very erratic, but I tried to keep my mouth shut and not show her how nervous I felt. What I was thinking was, "What the fuck am I doing here?"

My new wife's relatives looked at me and shuddered. At least that's what I imagined. My long hair and scraggly goatee probably did not endear me to them. Cathy's grandfather, a stooped over old farmer, took one long look at me and turned away. He never spoke to me the whole time I was there. Everything and everybody seemed totally foreign to my experience, which they were. When I tried to tell C how uncomfortable I was feeling, she stiffened. "Just try to be friendly. That might help."

"No one's trying to be friendly to me."

"Of course they are. You just won't let them." C shook her head. "Cousin Warren asked if you want to help with the milking."

"Cousin Warren? You call him Cousin fucking Warren? What is this, Dogpatch?"

"What should I tell him?" She stood there with her hands on her hips.

"What would I have to do?"

"You just follow Warren. Do what the rest of them do." She seemed to soften a little. "It's not that big a deal, sweetie." In that moment I thought I could learn to like her.

The milking was a big deal – for me. I'd never been up close to a cow. Cows were something I saw out the window of my father's car as we drove to the Jersey Shore. But here I was now in West Virginia in a barn full of cows and these mothers were huge and they were all crowding into the barn, bumping into each other like giant school kids. They paid no more attention to me than they did to the walls. I was sure I was going to be crushed to death. Cousin Warren and the other guys, a couple of hooded teenagers, didn't look concerned at all about the stampeding cows, so I tried not to either. The thing about the cows I began to realize was that even though they must have weighed a thousand pounds each, they could be pushed around. They were like big children. I could push on their fat haunches and they'd go in the direction I pushed, which by following Cousin Warren's lead, I saw was into the rows of milking stalls. There one of the high school boys piled feed into a trough in front of them and the other kid swung a gate down over their heads which locked them into place. It was a pretty efficient process and I breathed out hard and tried to relax once I saw that all the cows were immobilized

Warren finally spoke to me. He was a big guy and he stood ramrod straight in his big black rubber boots. I looked down at my own flimsy Converse high tops, which were now unrecognizable as anything but clumps of muck. "You ready to try your hand at milking?"

"What the fuck," I said. "I'm here."

The schoolboys started to chuckle, but Warren cut them a look and they stopped. "No call for cussing."

"So what do I do?" I wasn't about to apologize. I just wanted to get this thing over without totally humiliating myself.

"Well, come on over here then." He pointed to the ass end of a nearby cow. "You got to clean it first."

"Clean what?" I stared at the cow's butt.

"Here." Warren knelt down and wiped the cow's bulging udder with a piece of damp cloth. "Think you can handle that, boy?"

I bristled at the "boy" but nodded. "I'm good," I said.

Warren handed me the rag and a bucket of disinfectant that smelled worse than the cow crap. "You clean, I'll hook 'em up right after you. We'll work right on down the line."

The work wasn't too bad once I got into the rhythm of it. I'd swoosh down each cow, running the cloth over their sack and along each long round nipple. Then

Cousin Warren would zip in and attach the chrome milking machine's hoses to each tit. There was something kind of soothing about it. Even with all the nasty smells and rushing to stay ahead of ole Warren, I felt good about what we were doing by the time we finished the line. I was looking forward to seeing C and telling her all about it.

"We're not done here, boy." Cousin Warren brought me out of my reverie. "Not by a long shot."

"Look, man, I'd prefer it if you didn't call me boy."

"We still have to get them off the milkers. Swab 'em down again and move these gals back in to the pasture." I must have looked unhappy. "Course you can go on back if you want."

I wanted. My back was aching and the smell of the cow shit was starting to make me sick. "I'm fine," I said. "Let's get it done." Warren nodded and moved off down the line. I pulled my sneakers out of the muck and followed him.

THEY HAD THEIR BIG meal in the middle of the day down there, after all the morning work had been done. It felt good to sit down at the table with the others knowing that I'd worked hard. The long slab table was packed with food that the women had prepared. There were loaves of fresh baked bread and soft butter and a big pot of stewed chicken, and salad with hunks of fresh tomatoes. Cathy was laughing and smiling as she walked along behind all us menfolk, filling up plates and urging more food on everyone. I'd never seen her like this before. I kept shoveling the food into my mouth, but I was thinking about something else. I looked up once and saw Cousin Warren staring at me, like he was trying to figure something out. I nodded at him and he nodded back.

The women served coffee and tall glasses of milk for the teenagers, whose names and relationships I still didn't know and didn't much care about. The food was good, the coffee was hot, but it was time to leave. That much was clear to me. But I'd have to convince C of that first.

"I really want to stay longer," Cathy said when I finally got her off from the others. We were sitting in the front porch swing.

"But we've got a long way to go to get to Mexico. It's still about a three or four day drive to the border at Laredo."

"It's not like there's anyone waiting for us there."

"The whole point is to go to Mexico. This was just a side trip. That's what we decided."

"That's what you decided. You never even asked me."

"We talked a lot. I showed you all the maps and everything."

"There's a difference between talking and discussing. You just do what you want to do. You never ask me what I want." She stopped and turned to face me. "I don't think I want to go to Mexico." She said it too loud. "Not today, not ever."

"What are you saying? I thought we had a plan."

"Well, that's where you were wrong, Butchie boy."

"But what about the book?"

"What book?"

"*Mexico on Five Dollars a Day.* It's got all our plans. Where we're gonna stay and everything."

"Go on and get it," she said. "I wanta take a look at that book."

"Okay, good. Now you're talking." I ran to the VW and got the book from the back seat and brought it back to the porch and handed it to C. Now we could make a plan together, if that's the way she wanted it. I could learn.

Cathy held the book up and looked at the cover like she'd never seen it before. Then she opened the Mexico book up. And started tearing out the pages. Tearing them out in big, ragged clumps and throwing them off the porch. Throwing those pages every which way – and smiling.

Up in Flames

Moving to Cambridge had been a bad idea right from the start. Or maybe getting married to Cathy when we hardly knew each other was the bad idea. It was my fault, no sense blaming her. What good would that do? I wanted someone to take care of me, someone who looked presentable and that's about as deep as I took it.

I must have thought going to Harvard would change my life – or our life. And maybe it did. I mean, I loved going to my graduate school classes. It was the first time in my life I truly felt inspired by education, felt I was part of the process, really growing as a person. But then I'd come home to our squalid little apartment in East Cambridge, and try to tell my wife about the amazing class I'd sat through with Robert Coles or John Holt, and she'd just stare off into space and smile.

The weekend after the first term was complete, we planned to take a trip back to Philly to see some old friends and my family. We decided to take the Greyhound cause a storm was being predicted with lots of snow. And when it snows in Massachusetts, it really snows. Before we left, I went down to the car, a Volkswagen Beetle, which I had bought for myself as a college graduation present. If a person can truly love an inanimate object, I loved that vehicle. Yeah, it was slow, and the heater never kept you warm enough, but it had a sun roof, that rolled back with a hand crank, and a handle down under the dash that would give you an extra gallon of gas if you ran out, so you never had to worry. I locked it up, even though I didn't think anyone would bother stealing such an inexpensive car. Just then a couple of the neighborhood kids walked up to me. They couldn't have been much older than 10 or 12. "Hey, mister," the taller, dark-haired kid said, "You want us to watch your car? You know, make sure it's safe and all."

"No," I said, hardly giving it a thought. "I'm good."

"Well, you never know," the kid said. "Some bad people in this neighborhood."

I thought about what we'd discussed in some of my ed school classes. "People aren't really bad or good. They just respond to the circumstances they're born into."

"Yeah, well whatever," the boy said. "It's only a dollar a day."

"No" I said again, "But thanks for asking."

I think they might have been laughing when they walked off.

I told Cathy about the encounter with the kids. But she only said, "Well, it's your car. I guess you can do whatever you want." We gathered our stuff together and went off to catch the bus for the long ride south. As we walked out the door, and down the street, I took one last look at my beautiful little Bug. Everything will be fine, I told myself. It will all work out.

The week in Philadelphia drove C and I even farther apart. It wasn't any one particular thing. If asked, I could come up with a whole string of complaints. As, I'm certain, could she. But nobody was asking. Not our friends and not my family. They all acted as if our unhappy marriage was invisible. Even my mother, never one to hold her tongue, didn't have anything to say about her prodigal son and his *shiksa*.

Maybe going to Harvard had finally won her over. But I doubted that. In fact, when I had first told my parents about my acceptance, Mom said, "See, that proves you could have gone to medical school." I didn't quite follow her reasoning, but decided to say nothing. Growing up with my mother's out-size expectations, going silent had become my go-to defense. If I had been more thoughtful I might have seen that I was now doing the same thing with my wife. We spent the major portion of our time together that week, including 10 hours of riding the bus, in near-silent mode. I didn't know if I was angry with her or if she was angry with me. It was a pointless exercise. And I was feeling old and world-weary way before my time.

As we traversed the final miles on the bus back to Cambridge, I decided that I had to put an end to our misery. I knew it would be a difficult conversation to have, but also felt clear (finally) that I couldn't allow the situation to continue. Maybe C would have something to say that would change my mind, but I doubted it. I looked over at her then, curled up on the bench seat, peacefully asleep, and felt for a moment an affection for her, and a sadness for what we were about to lose. Cathy sat up and rubbed her eyes. "Are we close?" she asked.

"Almost there," I said, and reached over to touch her shoulder.

Cathy was the first to see it. "Look, is that your car?" We were walking up the street toward our apartment, weary from the long trip. I wanted only to get inside and collapse on to the couch. She pointed. "Over there. Isn't that where you left it?"

"No. I don't think so." There was only a heap of green metal where she was pointing. "Can't be. You know what my car looks like."

"Well, don't get mad at me," she said. "You're the one."

"The one what?" It all came into focus then. Charred black streaks crisscrossed the once shiny green metal. And there was the sunroof, now twisted open. The tires were melted into the asphalt of the street. My car had clearly been set on fire, and left to burn. "What the fuck happened here?" I screeched.

"I think you know," she said. "I'm sorry, Butch. But you should have thought this through."

"Now what do I do?"

"Come on inside," she said, and took my arm, gently pulling me away from the ruined car. "I'll make you a cup of hot chocolate. Maybe we can talk."

I shook my head, trying to clear the frustration and the anger, then looked at Cathy. "Something has to change," I said.

"I know," she said. "It does."

The House on Baltimore Avenue

It was a red brick duplex with a wide front porch and a set of concrete steps that led down to Baltimore Avenue. I'd grown up in this house, though now I lived in an apartment building a couple miles away, kind of a shitty place, but adequate. It was close to the school where I worked as an English teacher. My wife was six or seven months pregnant and we had talked about how it would be good to have a nicer place to bring the baby home to.

I always thought the house on Baltimore Ave was a great place, even felt proud to live there. I especially liked that there were three flights of wooden stairs that I could jump down when my father wasn't around. I had it worked out so that I could make it down all three flights in four dare-devilish leaps. Made me feel like Superboy. It wasn't a big fancy house. Not like my friend Joe Cohen's house, which was an actual mansion, with a tennis court and a regulation size backboard and hoop where we played endless games of pick up basketball. Our house had only a tiny backyard where the dirt was hard and full of gravel and nothing could ever grow. The Cohens moved out of the neighborhood in 1956 and fled to the suburbs like all the rest of the well-to-do Jewish families in West Philadelphia, because they were scared of the Black families moving in. But not my dad. At least not back in the fifties or sixties. But by 1970 he was ready to go too and decided to sell our house.

His car had been broken into a couple of times as it sat parked out on the street in front. Thieves stole the battery one time, and then after he replaced it, they stole the new one. Nobody had garages in our neighborhood. Houses weren't built like that, no room when you had to squeeze in a bunch of buildings on one city block. Unwisely, Dad then decided to go out and buy himself a brand new automobile – a jet black Chevrolet Impala. I was shocked. My dad did not own cool cars. There had been a '49 Frazier and a gray '54 Buick and a couple other sedate sedans. But this Impala was a great looking car, the kind with flaring rear fins and a big engine and, though he would never admit it, Dad was excited about owning such a sharp vehicle.

And then – you know what's coming, don't you? He parked the car out on the street, as usual, turned on the TV, watched his shows, went to bed, woke up, looked out the bedroom window and saw only an empty space where the black Chevy had sat. That morning he and

Mom decided they'd had enough and put the house up for sale.

I tried to argue against it, but I had no standing in this decision. My objections were half-hearted in any case. My parents were getting old and they deserved to have a more relaxed life, in a place where they felt safe. Forget about what that "right" thing to do was. Dad was nearing retirement and Mom had been pestering him for years to move to New Jersey where many of her friends now lived. Dad was finally ready to agree, but I sensed that it was still with some reluctance and maybe even a sense of defeat. He hadn't wanted to be like all the others, a part of the "white flight." My dad had his principles. They were observable in his actions, if not in his speech. Dad didn't speak very much at all. At least not to me, or to anyone else in the family, including Mom. I guess he believed in the dignity of silence, that if one wanted to be heard, it was necessary to say only what was deathly important, like John Wayne. Dad and I had only a few conversations when I was "under his roof." Most of them were short, and about sports. We did have one meaningful talk. I turned to him when I was hurting about a girl. It meant a lot to me at the time, thirteen years old and broken hearted over Carolyn Blattner who dumped me for Crazy Joey down the block. Dad put his arm around my shoulder and told me there would be lots of girls to come after Carolyn and he took me seriously and never laughed. I wish there had been more talks like that. But there weren't.

Distance builds walls over time and then you reach a point where there's no climbing over. Hey, I gave up too. Trying to talk to him was too hard. All I could manage was to make him angry. Maybe that was what I was trying to do. By the time I was out of college and living a life of my own, we barely noticed one another.

Mom and Dad decided they would move to Cherry Hill, New Jersey, right across the Ben Franklin Bridge, but about eight million miles away from West Philly. My sister already lived there, with her new husband in a house with a swimming pool. "Regulation Olympic size," the husband informed me. My parents were moving into a condominium. Essentially, they were buying an apartment in a huge block of a building full of other apartments. Mom said it was "very snazzy." I'll have to admit, I wasn't allowing any of my reactions to affect me very much. I wouldn't have wanted to live in a condo in Cherry Hill, but what the hell, I was not them.

What I did think, however, was – Hey, I could live in the old family house. It was all instinct at first. The idea leapt into my thoughts as if radioed in by some outside force field. It would be great to have a real house to bring the baby home to. And the price was right. Even I could probably afford the cut rate, flee-the-neighborhood price my dad was asking. It would be weird, sure. It would mean that my wife and I would move into my parents' bedroom – could I get over that? Make love there? But we'd make the place our own. Tear down some walls, use a shit load of paint, take up the shag carpet my mother was so proud of. Cathy was all for it. So, I approached my father. Heart in my mouth.

I caught him outside the old house, as he was getting in his rental car. He was leaving for work, dressed the same way he was always dressed, with a jacket and tie, overcoat, and drab brown hat. The uniform of his day.

"Hey Dad," I called to him. "Could I talk to you about something?"

"I don't have much time." Dad looked at me like I was a stranger. "What do you want?"

"Well, I was thinking," I stumbled on.

"Yes?"

"I was thinking maybe Cathy and I could buy your house."

He stared at me like my teeth had just spontaneously fallen out of my mouth.

"I mean this house, our house," I said, pointing to the front porch. "Why not, huh?"

"Are you crazy, boy?" He got into the car, shaking his head, rolled down the window, and said, "You're in no position to own a home."

I was stunned. I didn't expect him to leap for joy, but I didn't expect this curt dismissal either. I backed off; Dad slammed the car door and looked straight ahead. I stood there while he started it up and drove away.

Strangely, I didn't feel angry; it was all too shameful for that. What I thought was: He's right. Stupid asshole boy.

I never said another word about it. Not to my wife or my mother, or my father, of course. I just swallowed it, made it part of that dark place inside of myself that struggled for the next 40 years to make sense of who I was and why I had so much trouble trying to breathe.

IT WAS ON A summer trip back to the old neighborhood in

2008 that the incident came back to me. I had brought my new wife to Philadelphia, to show her where I had grown up. It was remarkably the same. Sure, Ringers Pharmacy was now a coffee house, and Berman's grocery an upscale restaurant, but otherwise, the houses remained largely the same, the trees in Clarks Park still full and pretty. Even our old house was in much the same shape as I remembered it, though without the M. Freedman, M.D. sign on the front porch. I told Bev then about wanting to buy the place way back when, laughing self -consciously still at what a fool I'd been. "It was really stupid of me," I told her.

"Why?" she said. "This looks like it would have been a great house to raise a family in?"

"You think?"

"Sure, and a great investment too. What did your dad sell the place for?"

"Ten thousand."

"Incredible," she chuckled. "What do you think it's worth now?"

"Three hundred."

"At least," Bev said.

"Yeah, that's right," I said. "Maybe I wasn't such an idiot after all."

"Maybe not," she said. Then we walked over to the old drug store and had a cup of coffee.

When She Was Born

I remember when my daughter Jessica was born. How could I forget? It was a difficult time in my life – a time I was too stupid and self-involved to even realize how fucked up everything was. And, of course, it was even more difficult for my wife – for Catherine. But I didn't know much of what was going on for her. She didn't say and I didn't ask. Probably because I wouldn't have known what to do with the answer.

We were both young. Way too young to be married, to be having a child, to have to act like adults and be responsible, be smart, even kind. But there I was, a 25-year-old man/boy with a massively pregnant and unhappy wife. Now maybe we had figured things wrong – it wouldn't have been the first time – but according to our calculations Catherine was way overdue – almost a month. Each added day the pressure built. We would sit in the dark living room of our Philadelphia apartment, trying not to look at one another, waiting for something to happen.

"Are you sure it hasn't started?" I said. "Maybe you're just not feeling it."

"Don't be an idiot," Cathy said, looking stringy-haired miserable. "You think I won't know when I go into labor." Her face turned a blotchy purple, like it always did when she was angry.

"Don't call me an idiot."

"Well, you are one," she said with a withering look, and heaved herself off the couch and waddled to the bedroom, slamming the door behind her.

I lit a Marlboro and pretended that I was some other person, someone more like the guy I thought I was going to be when I left college. That guy was traveling all over the world, writing, meeting people, having adventures. Laughing like a goddamn loon for no reason. Too bad that guy wasn't me. The me who was teaching English in the worst high school in the city, hating every minute of it because I had no friends and no particular ambition and blamed my wife for just about everything because she was a handy target. I felt like I had driven my car off the side of the road and all I could do was watch the steering wheel spin around.

When we moved into this apartment in a not-so-great section of West Philly Catherine had gone out and bought yards and yards of a heavy velvet fabric in a deep purple shade that looked like spilled wine, and proceeded to make drapes to cover every window in the place. She said it made her feel safe, but it mostly made me feel creepy, like we were crouched down and hiding in a bunker, which might have been okay (even funny) if I'd been hiding with someone I got along with.

Finally it did happen. The contractions began and we hurried out to the little Ford Falcon parked outside on the street. The car Catherine's father had given us with the admonition to me to be "really careful of this vehicle. It's a damn classic." And then the first day I parked it in front of the apartment some kids from the school had busted out the taillights and left a note that said, *fuck you, teach*. And as long as I'd anticipated this moment, as many times as I'd rehearsed what to do – damn, we'd even gone to Lamaze classes – once the real thing was on us, I was completely surprised. Could this really be happening?

It felt like we were in an episode of The Twilight Zone. I would not have been at all surprised to see aliens leap out of my wife's mouth, which was at the moment twisted in a blood-curdling scream, then punctuated with the kind of profanities my students used on the basketball court.

During the delivery Cathy screamed at me – words I'd never heard cross her middle-class, college girl lips before. "Get your fucking hands off me, asshole!" It made me smile at the same time it scared the hell out of me. What had possessed her? I hung in there and fed her ice chips, no matter the names she called me. The doctor, who had looked at me warily beforehand, told me I was a trooper. I guessed that was a good thing. And when the baby finally appeared, slid out into the world, I knew that nothing could ever be the same. Right from that moment the world was full of love and danger and I knew that my new job was all about protecting my daughter. The nurses whisked her away before we even had much of a chance to hold her or count her toes.

Something was wrong. I sensed that, though nobody was talking and Cathy was now too drugged up to protest. I demanded to know what was happening. Where was my daughter and why were people acting so weird? I might be a skinny hippy boy, but I knew when someone was messing with me. What I was being told was that they, the hospital – had everything under control. There were some, uh, minor problems, but that I shouldn't worry about them and should instead stay with and comfort my wife and they would let me know what I needed to know when I needed to know it. I went batshit crazy. "You can't do this. Let me see my daughter. Right this damn minute or tell me why." The nurses had to restrain me from pushing my way into the I.C.U. The doctor was called to calm me down. I wasn't leaving until the baby was shown to me.

"Okay, okay." He relented and led me in to see me my daughter, now hooked up to tubes and with a strange yellow cast to her skin. I was dumbstruck, scared. He explained that the condition was not unusual and could be corrected in a day or two. There were names and terms he used that I no longer remember – jaundice was among them. I said I wouldn't leave until she was okay. He said I couldn't do that. I said, "Sorry, man, but I'm not going anywhere," and crossed my arms over my chest. He called security, two beefy guys, who moved me forcibly out of the room and escorted me out of the hospital.

I was out of my mind. I wandered around the

streets of downtown Philadelphia for a while and then called my father, a doctor himself, who I rarely spoke to, but now it seemed like he was the only one who would know what to do. He told me to take a deep breath, go back to the hospital, and stay there as long as I needed to. "Just wait and watch," he said. "Be respectful. No shouting. No one is trying to hurt your daughter. This will all work out." And he was right.

We brought Jessie home in a couple days, healthy and squalling, and before long we had forgotten all the trauma of her birth, so involved were we with the miracle of her being in our lives and so scared of all the new responsibilities. I was amazed that we were able to do this – be parents. Even if there were days when I still felt like a child myself, now that had to be put to the side. It was time to grow up.

Rescue

Jessica is still a baby. Maybe nine months old. And she cries every night. Loud, pathetic wails. She doesn't stop until Cathy or I go to her. Then we either sit with her, rocking and cajoling till she falls back asleep – for another few hours – or we bring her into the bed with us. The bed is easier, as then the baby will sleep through the night and we can get some rest. It's an old story and we have received much advice from parents and well-meaning friends. Most sing the same tune: "Let her cry. Eventually she'll stop. You just have to tough it out." But neither my wife or I seem able to go there. Jessie's our first and we are madly in her thrall. We can sit for hours just watching her. She has been the glue to patch our cracked and crumbling marriage.

"Don't you think it would be traumatic if we just let her cry?" Cathy asks over our morning coffee. It has been a long, largely sleepless night, and now I have to go to work.

"Who knows?"

"Well, we have to do something."

"I guess." The coffee is black and bitter the way I like it.

"Do you want to try tonight?"

"I don't want to try," I say. "If we're gonna do it we need to just do it. No fucking around."

"Fine," Cathy says. "No fucking around." Then I pick up my lunch sack that she has filled for me and go out the door.

It starts around 10 o'clock that night. Jessie went down at eight. The cries are piercing, mournful, alarming. She barely stops to take a breath. I lie rigid in bed, staring at the drop-down ceiling. Cathy pretends to read a book. It goes on for 20 minutes, feels like 20 years. It would be so easy to go to her, comfort her, comfort me. But we made a deal. And I'm big about keeping my end of deals. Then there's the future. It has to stop somewhere. I mean, we all have to figure this out together. "Damn," I say to Cathy, "I'm going nuts."

"Me too," she says.

"We need to hang on," I say.

"Okay."

I clench my jaws together. Cathy goes back to reading. The baby continues to scream. I want to scream myself. How did all this shit happen anyway?

I only last another 20 minutes, maybe 15. I don't know. All I know is that I have to go to that child. She needs me. "That's it." I bounce off the bed. "Something might be wrong," I tell Catherine.

"I understand," she says, as I run out of the bedroom.

Jessie stops crying the instant I pick her up and hold her warm little body to me.

I GLANCE OUT THE front window. I'm checking once again on my five-year-old daughter, who is out playing with the other little girls in the neighborhood. What a beautiful child, I think. She makes all the other kids seem dull, as if they've been painted in a lesser hue. Then I see Kelly, the neighbor's kid and Jessica's best friend, slap her hard across the face. I almost can't believe what I'm watching. Jessie begins to cry; she doesn't defend herself. The other girls are laughing and teasing her, pulling at Jessie's jacket. My immediate and overwhelming impulse is to rush out the front door and rescue her and, in the process, to grab the awful Kelly and shake her until her teeth rattle. But I hold back. She's got to learn to deal with this kind of thing on her own, I tell myself. Then I see Kelly hit her again and I'm flying out the door.

WHEN SHE'S EIGHT YEARS old Jessica falls off the roof. I watch the whole thing happen. It's a low roof, maybe twelve feet high at the ridge and not too steep. She and her buddy Noah discover that they can climb through the bedroom window and be out on the rooftop, free as little birds. We are having a barbecue that afternoon and I am cooking burgers and corn on the cob, drinking beer. A hot summer day, everyone is in a festive mood. Kids are running around yelling; the adults are talking, joking, passing around a joint. When I look up from the grill to see Jessie and Noah walking around on the roof,

I'm, for some reason, not particularly concerned. They blend in to everything else. Jess is backing up, away from Noah. They are giggling, play fighting with imaginary swords. Jess keeps edging backwards and before I can make sense of it, I know what is going to happen. She takes a last step and plunges off the edge. It's like a slow-motion film; she doesn't have time even to scream. The thud of her landing takes both our breaths away. Jessica makes no sound when I reach her. Her eyes are closed; she is unconscious. I can't help thinking she is dead. I'm too scared to know what to do. Noah's mother, Ruth, moves to her side. Ruth is a naturopathic physician. She pushes gently on Jessie's skinny chest and then blows air into my daughter's mouth. Jessie's eyelids flutter open and she returns. She even smiles. I hug her to me and start to breathe again. Not even a broken bone. The party continues.

IN HIGH SCHOOL, JESSICA runs track. She is very good and I am unhealthily proud of her. But I am too involved, a pushy parent. Her coach finds something else to do when I show up at workouts. Jess has grown tall and leggy, a natural distance runner. Even as a freshman she wins races. I know I'm crowding her, but don't know how to stop. At her meets I scream like a deranged person. "Run Jess, run. You can do it. Dammit, go! Go, go, go!" The other parents look away from me. I ask Jess later if she can hear me while she's running. She rolls her eyes. "How could I not?" Junior year she goes to State and finishes third, recording a school record in the 3,000 meters. Senior year is going to be big, I decide. I've talked to her about what she has to do to win an athletic scholarship. The coach from the University of Oregon has already scouted her. But that last year her body changes. Full puberty has been late in coming, perhaps delayed by the many miles of training. The transformation now is like a betrayal. Hips and breasts change her stride, slow her down. We are finding it hard to talk. I don't know what to say to her. Maybe I am more concerned about myself, my own disappointments. Maybe. But it's also more than that.

We've reached the point where I have to admit she's no longer my little girl. Jess, I'm sure, has long ago reached this conclusion. No matter how hard I cheer for her or train with her, she is not going to be the same lithe runner she once was. I try to talk to her, but it doesn't go well.

"Maybe you could try some other events. Maybe the sprints, or the shot put."

"I'm not a shot putter. And I'm not a sprinter."

"You could be."

'No, I couldn't."

"Well, you could try."

(Silence)

Jessie doesn't quit the team, and I'm proud of her for that. She keeps running the 1500 and 3000 meter events, but her times are significantly slower than they were the year before. From what I can tell she doesn't much care about her times. I notice when I drop by the practice field, that she spends most of the workout chatting with her buddies and flirting with the boys. The coach doesn't seem to mind. I suppose he's seen this all before. When I ask him about my daughter, he just shrugs. "She'll find something else," he says. I feel like punching him in the face, but turn and walk back toward the track. Jess won't even look in my direction.

At the district meet she quits running after two laps and sits down on the cinder track, head in her hands, as the other runners flash by. In the stands I jump up, ready to run onto the field. I have to save her, somehow. I start down the steps, then pull back and sit in a different seat. I can't go to her now. It would only embarrass her further.

Going home in the car, Jessica breaks into tears. "Why do I screw everything up?" she blubbers.

"You don't," I tell her. "Don't even think that."

"But it's true," she says. "Nothing ever goes right for me."

"Things will get better," I tell her. "Believe me."

She still cries all the way home.

WHEN JESS RETURNS FROM her freshman year at college, we take a family trip to the Oregon Coast. I decide it is a good time to have a talk with her – about school, and about her plans for the future. I imagine a pleasant conversation, sitting in easy chairs, staring out at the ocean, drinking hot chocolate. I've learned some things in my life. And I'd really like to tell my daughter about them. If she'll only give me a chance. When was the last time I held her hand? Today I notice that she is now slightly taller than I am.

The conversation does not go as I pictured it. It's late in the day now and we can no longer see out the fogged windows. Jess is sprawled on the couch reading a book, though it doesn't look like a textbook. Might even be some sort of mystery novel. I find myself getting irritated and try to rein it back. Do I really think my daughter's choice of reading material is a reflection on me? Don't be so damn judgmental, I tell myself at about the same instant that I realize I can't help it. I judge all the fucking time, even with myself, especially with myself. I take a few deep breaths. Cleansing breaths. That's what they call it in the yoga class, which I've started taking to help me stay centered, or something like that. "Breathe, Butch," I tell myself, apparently out loud.

"What'd you say?" Jess looks up from her novel.

"Nothing. Just a cough."

She closes her book and sits up. Hitches up her baggy sweat pants.

"Going to bed?" I ask.

"Yep."

"It's only 10 o'clock. Thought you college kids were night owls."

"Night owls?"

"Yeah, you know, staying up till all hours, talking, philosophizing, shooting the shit."

"I'm tired now," she says.

"I thought maybe we could talk." I say it in a rush; spit it out like a bad taste.

"About what?" She stops but doesn't turn around.

"About whatever we want."

"And what would that be?"

"Well, what do you want to talk about?"

"I don't."

"Not anything at all?"

"Not really."

I just thought that maybe there were some things at school you might be concerned about?"

"Concerned?" She sounds aggrieved, but I push on.

"Yeah, concerned. You know, like you're troubled about something. Maybe some of your classes are difficult, or the place where you live isn't what you want it to be."

"Everything's fine, Dad. Seriously."

"Okay, then. Good, as long as there's no problem."

"No problem."

"Well, good night, then."

"Okay," she says and walks off to the bedroom she's sharing with her sister.

When she's gone I slam my fist on to my knee, then I return to my dumbass breathing exercise.

NOW, 20 YEARS LATER, Jess has come to stay with us for a couple weeks. She's not sure how long exactly. She's between jobs, the last one working as a trimmer on a marijuana farm. She's applying to graduate school in social work. She'd like me to help her with the application essay, she tells me which I'm more than happy to do. "Graduate school would be good for her, don't you think?" my wife Bev asks. "It would give her a new focus."

"Yeah, definitely." I say. I love how supportive Bev is, always happy when Jessie comes to visit. Even talks and laughs with her in a way I no longer can. "I hope she follows through."

WHEN JESS WAS STILL a baby, I used to carry her everywhere

I went in a carrier on my back. I loved the feel of her wiggling little body against mine, even when she got heavy. We'd walk on the beach, and down to the bay front, and later to the grocery store. Sometimes I'd buy a Hershey bar and as we returned to the house reach back over my shoulder to give her one of the little squares of chocolate, knowing that she would make a mess and end up with chocolate smears all over herself and the backpack, but I couldn't resist the squeals of her delight, couldn't resist making her happy. How easy it was. How perfect. We could always clean up the mess later.

Before Jessie leaves, we go to a coffee shop to work on the graduate school application essay. I've already read a rough draft and made extensive edits and comments on it. When we've settled into a booth, coffees in front of us, small talk exhausted, I put the heavily marked up essay on the table.

"Wow, you really tore into it," she says.

"Well, I figure it's important to get it right. Important to you."

She's holding the pages up in front of her. "Is it really that bad?"

"No, not bad at all. It just needs to flow better, make better transitions between your points. A lot of the corrections are grammatical, or typos."

"Yeah, I don't get it about that whole comma thing," she says. "I just sorta take a handful and throw them at the page and see where they stick."

I laugh. "Yeah, well there are some rules." I am relieved that she is not taking offense. "Want to go over it line by line? I'll show you what I was thinking. You get to decide whether you want to change anything or not. It's your essay."

"You're sounding like a teacher, Dad."

"That's my deal."

"I'm glad," she says. Then, after a moment of quiet, "You know, I really appreciate this."

"It's nothing," I say. Something in me lets go then. My daughter no longer needs rescuing, I think. Nor do I.

Part Four

Trying to Find Home

Changing Tides

Moving back to Long Beach Island, New Jersey as an adult was, of course, my idea. But Cathy was willing, and we had a young daughter to consider now. I told C that I could get work there, though I had no idea how, and that we could rent a place on the cheap. Strangely enough, it all worked out. That wasn't how I was used to things going for me then. But we found a nice house to rent (I think it was $85 a month), and I started commercial clamming for a living. It wasn't what I had expected to be doing with my life when I graduated college, but it wasn't bad. Not bad at all.

The first thing I'd do each morning was climb the stairs to an outside deck where I could catch a look at Barnegat Bay, to see if there were any whitecaps visible, a sign that the wind was blowing hard and that working the bottom might be difficult that day. But as March rolled into April, the morning air would become softer, almost sweet. It was on those days that

I felt filled with a quiet joy, a contentment that I've rarely felt since. The day on the water, working alone and working hard, stretched in front of me with a welcoming nod. I felt connected, without knowing exactly to what or why or even caring about giving it words. It was enough to be, to drink my coffee and walk on down to the boat. I hadn't discovered meditation back then, but if I had I might have noted that how I felt was the state that all meditators aspire to.

The object in clamming was to catch as many clams as possible in any given day, then haul them back, sorted by size into burlap bags, and drop them off at the clam buyer's shed. Two hundred clams to a bag; five full bags made for a good day's pay. Five cents per clam was the going rate, but it could vary depending on the market. Each bag weighed well over a hundred pounds, but I didn't worry about that. It felt good to sling the heavy sacks off the deck of the boat onto the dock. By the time I drove my flat-bottomed wooden work boat (a garvey) back to where I kept it moored in the bay, unloaded my equipment, and walked up 11th street to our little cottage, I was physically exhausted, but not beaten down. There's a big difference, you know. My back might ache, might have cramps in my hands, but my head was clear. I was never too tired to take a late evening stroll on the beach with my wife and our baby daughter.

A word, then, about catching clams. Maybe harvesting is the more accurate word, but what I heard around the docks was "catching." I didn't argue. There are two basic methods for East Coast clamming: treading and raking. (There's also tonging, but only a few old-timers still did that.) In treading, the clammer jumps over the side of the boat, wearing a wet suit, into shallow water (three or four feet deep) and treads backward along the bay bottom feeling for clams with his feet (I'd say his or her feet, but frankly I never came across a female clammer). When he feels one, a hard ridge in the muck, he dives down and picks it up. Some clammers have developed a technique of working the clam out of the mud and up their leg, so that they don't have to dive each time. I found it easier and quicker to dive. Repeat this process over a thousand times a day and you've got a fairly decent catch and a head full of salt water.

Raking is the method we switched over to once the water became too icy for treading. Even a wetsuit will only keep you so warm. The rake is used to pull along the bay bottom from the side of the boat. It has a head that's about four feet across and long sharp teeth that sluice through the mud. The handle extends to over twelve feet in length. Kind of a monster rake; it takes a strong back to keep working that baby through the muck all day long as the boat drifts through the shallows. Some times you can go hours pulling up nothing but mud, shells, and molting crabs; but then there are the times you find yourself over a rich bed. An experienced bayman can tell he's on it, by the ticki-tick-tick of the rake teeth as they slide over the clam shells. On board the clammer smiles, grunts, and digs the rake even deeper. With a final heave, he pulls the rake head to the gunwales, shakes it a few times in the water to wash away the mud, and pulls his rake head full of dark cherrystones on to the deck. Nothing feels better.

I had to give up clamming in 1976 when we moved to Seattle. My wife was tired of Long Beach Island,

New Jersey and its cold winters and isolation. In many ways the life of a bayman had not changed for hundreds of years. Except for the outboard motors, the rhythms were the same. We lived by the tides and the seasons. One long day after the next. It wasn't what Cathy had signed up for. She needed friends and a social life, wanted a place where people talked about things other than the next storm or when the bay would ice over. We had college friends in the Pacific Northwest. They told us it was lovely, that housing was cheap, that cool people were moving there in droves. I tried to hold out, tried to build a case for life on this six mile long island. I couldn't imagine selling my boat; I had just invested in a replacement motor, a spanking new 25 horsepower Johnson. But eventually I gave in. Seattle would be better for the children and C was now pregnant with our second. I couldn't be selfish is what I thought. I feel trapped, is what I thought. Goddamn it all, is what I thought. I'll tell you, I miss that boat to this day and think about it more often than seems natural.

In Seattle I put my education to use and found work once again as a high school teacher. It was a good job, paid enough to support our family of four, and allowed us to buy a nice old house in the Wallingford neighborhood. But somehow over the years my life became more complicated. Teaching and writing did not provide the same sense of being at one with the seasons and the tides. I no longer felt like my own man. Everybody had a piece of me now – students, administrators, parents. Though more secure, pension and health insurance in place, I ended up feeling tense and worried. The work life of a high school English teacher separated me from the throb of life by the sea, where the only imperative was to keep an eye on the horizon. And while the feeling at the end of a day on the bay was one of completion and exhausted satisfaction, the satisfactions, such as they were, of teaching were more nebulous. Who ever knew if you were doing the job correctly? It sometimes felt like steering without a tiller. Where is it we were all headed and how would we know when we arrived?

But there was no going back to the life of a clammer. That vocation was long behind me and, for the most part, had died away in my absence. Truth be told, it had been dying even back when I worked the bay. Near the end of my stay, more and more areas of Barnegat Bay and Little Egg Harbor were being closed to shellfishing because of pollution and the scarily named "Red Tide." My brother, who still lives in New Jersey, tells me that maybe a dozen old-timers still make a living raking clams there. What're you going to do? Time passes, but still I remember the days when I would get up in the morning and go out on the water and earn a living with hard work and an untroubled soul.

No Going Home

We drove from Seattle across the country jammed into our little Ford Fiesta. I did all the driving, while Cathy navigated. The two girls were snuggled into the back seat along with as many toys and games as we thought would keep them from screaming. I don't know what we thought would keep us sane.

I was 33 years old that winter and generally unhappy with my life. Nothing was as exciting or meaningful as I had imagined it would be. I felt, somehow, cheated. Though who was doing the cheating I couldn't have told you.

I convinced Cathy that we should move back East. I said that I wanted my children to grow up around family, to know their grandparents, which was true, but not accurate. My family was never very warm or welcoming to us – especially since Cathy was adamantly non-Jewish. She even tried once to convert my mother. That did not go well.

No, the real reason we were halfway through Kansas right now was that I felt lost, and I was dragging my family along on my quest to be found. That night we stayed in the cheapest motel we could find. The next morning the girls woke up scratching their scalps. A quick inspection confirmed the diagnosis – head lice. "Maybe we should shave their heads," I suggested. "Noooo, Daddy," Jessie, the older one, wailed. "Don't cut my hair."

Gabrielle, five years younger, started to cry.

"Okay, okay," I said. "Just get in the car." I thought about what my mother would say when we showed up at their immaculate house, complete with vermin.

"This whole thing is one big mistake," Cathy said then.

"Thanks for the support," I muttered.

We arrived in New Jersey, exhausted, irritable, and itchy, at the same time that a major snowstorm hit the coast. It felt to me symbolic, though I didn't know of what. I had arranged with my parents to use their summer cottage at the Jersey Shore. They had agreed, with some reluctance. When we had unpacked, and I had crawled under the house to turn on the water, I lit a fire in the fireplace, and we all huddled around the meager warmth. We sat the girls in front of us on kitchen chairs and went to work picking the nits out of their hair. There were hundreds of them. Later I called my parents to tell them we'd arrived. Dad picked up the phone, which was unusual. He usually let Mom do all the talking. "Well, we're back home," I said, "The girls are anxious to see you."

"So, you couldn't make it out there, could you," Dad said. "Another dead-end."

I felt my heart sink into my gut, "I wasn't thinking of it that way," I told him. "I thought you'd be pleased."

"So what will you do for work?"

"I haven't decided."

"You haven't decided? You're a grown man with a family to support."

"I know who I am, Dad."

"Sometimes I wonder, Butch."

"Can I speak to Mom now?"

"Don't forget to turn off the porch lights when you go to sleep." I pictured him handing the phone to my mother, a downturned scowl on his face, an expression I was all too familiar with.

"So you made it," Mom said by way of greeting.

"Yep, we made it. Just barely."

"What does that mean?"

"Well, the girls have a bit of a problem."

"Oh my god, what?" Mom said. "They're not sick, are they?"

"Not really."

"Not really? What are you talking about, Butchie?"

"Lice," I said.

"Lice! In their hair?"

"That's where they usually are."

"Don't get smart with me. I know what lice are. And I don't want them in my house."

"You don't want your granddaughters in your house?" My disappointment in my parent's lack of enthusiasm for our return was quickly morphing into something stronger and older. "Should we pack up and leave then?"

"Don't you put words in my mouth. I just didn't expect this."

"Neither did we." I could hear my father muttering in the background.

"Your father says that the lice will get into all the beds."

"And the furniture too," I heard Dad tell her.

"Look, we've spent the last three hours getting rid of them. I think they're all clean now."

"You think? That's not good enough, Butch."

"Well, the girls are asleep now. I can wake them up if you like and tell them we have to leave." Two could play at the guilt game. And I had been trained by the best. "Oh, and thanks for being so concerned about the girls. Yes, they were quite upset about the whole experience."

There was a pause then. I could hear the storm blowing outside and the slight crackle from the dying embers of the fire. Despite the current conversation, I remembered how much I loved this cottage and this place. It was weird, I thought, how I could hold both these worlds at once.

"Okay, look I'm sorry, honey. I over-reacted," Mom said. "Of course I'm concerned. Those poor girls."

"Yeah, It's been hard."

"I know. And I know you did your best."

"We stayed in a crummy motel. That's where they must have gotten them."

"Those places are not clean. I've always said that."

"We'll wash all the bedding tomorrow."

"And you'll call and tell us what's going on?"

"Sure, Mom."

"Okay, then, your Dad says goodnight."

"I know he didn't, but that's okay. He probably wanted to."

I hung up then and went to the window to look out on the snow-covered street. Tomorrow we'd trudge through the drifts up to the beach. The girls would like that. Later I would have to explain to them and to Cathy that it was time to leave again.

Busted

I defended them when they first got caught. I couldn't believe that they would do what this damn security guard was saying. Gabrielle was only six, and Jessica ten. I was outraged when the guard stopped us outside the Bi-Mart store. He grabbed Jessie's arm.

"Hey, what the hell are you doing?" I shouted. "Get your hand off of her." The girls looked as dumbfounded as I was. It was cold that day and they were wearing their puffy winter coats with attached hoods.

"Your girls were shoplifting in there," the guard said.

"Bullshit," I said. "My daughters don't steal."

"Then you won't mind if I search them." He was a big guy, with his belly rolling over the belt of his rent-a-cop outfit.

"You put one hand on either of them and I'm coming after you."

"Then I guess there's nothing left to do but call the police."

"Call the fuckin' police." I looked to the girls, confident of their innocence. They looked away.

"You'll have to come inside while we wait, sir."

I glanced at the girls again. Gay looked like she was about to cry. "Okay, screw it. Search them," I said. "But be careful how you do it."

It didn't take long. The security guard reached into the hood of Gabrielle's coat and pulled out a pink rubber ball and a tube of lipstick. He held them out to me. "I saw the big one drop them in there." Jessica stared down at the pavement.

"They didn't know what they were doing. I'll pay for the damn things." I felt my anger moving in a different direction.

"You're lucky this time," the guard said. "I'm not going to call the cops. But none of you will be allowed in this store from here on out. Am I understood?"

"Fuck you, man," I muttered, grabbed hold of the girls' hands and hustled them down the street. When I got them home, I told them to sit down at the kitchen table. "Why'd you do that?" Neither spoke. "You know we don't have to steal, don't you? I can buy you what you want."

"Not always," Jessie said.

"No, not always. That's right," I said. "But still you don't need to take things."

"I'm sorry, Daddy," Gay said.

"What about you, Jessie?"

"I didn't really take those things. They were in Gay's coat."

"You put them there," Gay said. "I didn't even know."

"Still," Jessie said. "I'm not the one."

"You are the one." I said. "At least admit what you did. Then we can move on here."

"You wouldn't have bought me the lipstick. I asked before."

"You don't need lipstick."

"Who says?"

"I do." I felt the situation slipping away from me. "I want you to go to your room and think about this. We're going to talk about stealing again in the morning."

"Me too, Daddy?" Gabrielle asked.

"You too what?" I snapped. Gay started to cry. Her big sister took her by the hand and led her upstairs to their bedroom. I sat down in my easy chair and turned on the television.

The next week, it happened again. We walked out of the Lucky Store on Greenwood Ave, me carrying two big paper bags of groceries, and Gabrielle trailing behind. As we walked back to our beat up old house, the one that didn't have any heat except the little trash burner in the kitchen, I noticed that Gay was chewing gum. "Where'd you get the gum?"

"I dunno." She was hanging on to my shirttails, the way she always did when we were out in traffic.

"You don't know where the gum in your mouth came from?"

"No, Daddy."

"Okay," I said. "We're going to figure this out when we get home."

By the time we got home, the damn grocery bags were wet and falling apart, and Gay had spit out her gum. She knew she was busted.

As I unpacked the groceries, Gabrielle stood by

the wood stove as if she was trying to get warm, even though there was no fire in it. I put the last bottle of milk in the fridge, then took the soggy bags and tore them into pieces and stuffed them into the stove.

"Want a fire?" I asked.

Gay nodded. She still hadn't taken her coat off.

"Wanta help me get the wood?"

She nodded again.

"Aren't you talking to me today?" I was feeling sad for her and for myself. I wanted a better life for both of us. And I didn't want to be mean to my kids, though sometimes lately I couldn't seem to help it. "I'm not mad at you, you know."

"You're not?" She looked up at me, and smiled.

Then I felt even shittier. "Come on, let's go out to the garage so I can cut up some wood."

"Are you going to use the buzz saw?"

"It's called a table saw."

"Why is it called that?" Gabrielle loved to ask questions. She would do it all day if you kept answering.

"Because it's mounted on a table."

But why is it called saw? What does saw even mean?"

"I don't know. I guess I never thought about it."

I pulled my jacket back on. It was even colder out in the garage, where I had stacked the wood pallets. I brought them home from the job I had in the warehouse of a book company. When people asked what I did for a living, I just said I worked in publishing. Gay sat on an old director's chair and watched while I worked. When I'd disassembled a couple pallets, I took the boards over to the table saw to cut them into short enough pieces to go into the stove. I put on my protective glasses and turned on the saw. The noise immediately filled up the garage. I could see why she called it a buzz saw. I didn't notice until too late that Gay had walked right up to the side of the table saw as I began pushing the boards through.

"Daddy, why does it make that sound?" I turned my head, barely able to hear, and saw her raise her hand toward the table and the spinning blade. Holding tight to the wood with my right hand, I swatted my daughter away with my left and felt the back of my hand connect with her face. I switched the motor off and took a deep breath. "Goddamn it, Gay. What the hell were you doing?" I looked down and saw that she was sitting on the garage floor, her face pale except for the pink streak where I had struck her. "You could have lost your hand. Don't you know that?" I bent to pick her up, pulled her up into my arms and held her tight. I'd never hit one of my children before. I must have started to cry.

"Don't cry, Daddy. I won't do it again."

We stood like that for another few minutes. I didn't want to let her go.

"Can we make the fire now?"

"Sure, baby. Let's go do that." I put her down and picked up a stack of kindling. "Let's go inside."

I made spaghetti and meatballs for dinner. It was the girls' favorite. During dinner Jessie told us some story about a boy in her class who was teasing her. "What'd you do then?" Gay asked. "I smacked him," Jessie said. "Right in the face."

"You shouldn't do that," I said. "There are better ways to handle things."

"But he wouldn't stop," Jessica said.

"You could have told the teacher, couldn't you?"

"No way. She just laughs and says, 'He's flirting with you'."

"Your teacher's a shithead," I said.

"Yeah, I know."

"Let's clear the table and do the dishes. Then we can talk about the other thing."

"What other thing?" Jessie asked.

"He means stealing stuff," Gay said.

"Oh that." Jessie looked down.

"Yeah, that," I said, wishing I had someone around to help me through this.

Jessica was in high spirits, still full of energy, talking non-stop. I think she was happy about standing up for herself that day in school and I was pleased that she'd been strong enough to deal with her problem, though I still didn't like the idea of her hitting some boy in the face.

"Okay, listen to me, now," I said. "There are certain things that are not okay to do. Do you guys understand what I'm talking about?"

"Sure," Jessie said. "That's like the ten commandments and all. Mom told us about them."

"Well, that's not exactly what I mean," I said, the mention of Cathy setting me back. My ex was now a committed churchgoer. "You don't have to believe in fairy tales to know the difference between right and wrong."

"But Mom says that we're all God's children and that we'll all go to heaven and be saved if we do right here on earth."

"That's why I don't like you going to see your mother. She's filling your heads with all that crazy bullshit."

"Mom says it's not okay to use swear words," Jessie said.

"Fuck Mom," I yelled.

The girls began to giggle, and I took a deep breath and tried to get back on track.

"Look, all I'm trying to say is that it's not okay to take things that don't belong to you. It's not only wrong, but it's illegal."

"What's ill-eagle?" Gay asked.

"It means it's against the law, dummy," Jessie said.

"Don't call her that."

"But she is," Jessie said. "She's stupid."

"Why don't you try to be nicer to your little sister," I said. "Anyway, I don't want this to ever happen again. If you want something or need something, you come and talk to me about it."

"But what if you don't have the money and we *really* need something? What then?" Jessie asked.

"Then I guess you just have to wait," I said. "You can't always have everything you want right when you want it."

"I wish I could," Jessie said.

I turned to Gabrielle, "So, where's the gum you got this afternoon?"

"It's upstairs in our room."

"Go get it," I said. She slid off her chair and ran upstairs. Jessica and I sat looking at each other while she was gone. I imagined she was thinking she'd rather be with her mother making cookies and listening to Jesus stories. I was glad when I heard Gay coming back down the steps. She put a yellow package of Chiclets on the table in front of me.

"So what are we going to do now?" I asked.

"I don't know," Gay said.

"I know," Jessie said, "we'll give them to poor people."

"Poor people don't need gum," I said.

"How do you know?" Jessie said, pushing her bottom lip out. She looked then just like her mother.

"That's not the point," I said. "Anyway, I want Gay to decide what she thinks we should do."

"I don't know," Gay said again, close to tears.

"What would be the right thing, baby? What might make you feel better?"

"I could take the gum back to the store," she said quietly.

"I think that's a good idea," I said.

"They're going to yell at her," Jessie chimed in. "And make her go to jail."

"No they're not." I said. I reached into my pocket and pulled out a dollar bill. "Take this with you. Give the gum and the money to the lady at the register, and tell her what you did." Gabrielle took the money and picked the gum up off the table. Looking at her frightened expression, it was all I could do to say, no, forget about it. Let's just all go watch television. "You go with her," I said to Jessica. "But let Gay do the talking." Jessie jumped up, glad now to have a part in what she probably saw as an exciting adventure.

After they'd bundled up and gone out the door, I went back into the kitchen to make lunches for the next school day. I opened the refrigerator door and stared inside it, but that's as far as I could get. "Damn," I said out loud. "Damn, damn, damn, damn." Then I went and sat back down at the kitchen table and waited for my precious daughters to come back home.

How to Get There from Here

The first time I came to the Oregon Coast was a sad affair, not one you'd think would presage my ongoing affection for the place. Cathy, and I and our two young daughters had just moved to Oregon from Seattle so I could take a teaching job in the small town of Banks. Banks is situated about 25 miles west of Portland in the foothills of the Coast Range. I didn't know why it was called Banks and was not curious enough to track down the answer. This was well before Google, you understand. Before even personal computers. Ancient times. Fucking 1982. The job and the move were necessary (not desired) as neither Cathy or I had any solid income prospects in Seattle. I'd been trying all summer to land a full-time teaching gig. I had hoped to find something closer to Seattle, where we had lived for the past seven years and had established a circle of friends and even owned a nice old Victorian style house that we bought on the cheap. Seattle was pretty laid back then. Easy to navigate, with beautiful mountains and lakes right in the damn city. We loved it there.

It was not easy to pack up and move. Sell our house in Wallingford, take the girls out of school, say goodbye to our close friends. We might as well have been moving to China. Sure, Banks was only 200 or so miles away. We could even come back to visit on weekends, we told ourselves. But, I think we knew that it probably wouldn't work that way. Once you're gone from a place, you're gone. Oregon, for better or worse, was now our new home. But I was glad to have the job. There were not many teaching gigs to be had back then – especially in Language Arts (the fancy name for an English teacher). And, why complain, Oregon was, after all a fine place to live and Banks, though rural and rough, was not without its charm. That is if you liked tractor pulls and road kill.

We found a place on the outskirts of town – town consisting of one long street, named, appropriately if unimaginatively, Main Street. Our rented home was at the end of a dirt road, not lovely at all. Scrub pines, abandoned vehicles, a road that was barely passable even in good weather. Where would I do my jogging, I wondered. How could I ride my 10 speed to work? The girls, and Cathy, seemed, though, to like the place. There was plenty of room for them to roam around, and Cathy immediately planted a garden and the girls each had their own room. The advantage I saw was that Banks was not far from the Coast – only about fifty miles straight west on Highway 6. My head filled with images of breaking surf and fresh air, walks on the sand and watching the pelicans swoop overhead. In Washington, trips to the Coast had been our release. I had bought a used pick-up camper complete with a mini kitchen, fold-down table, and a cozy bunk for the girls that poked out above the cab of the '69 International. We made many trips in that old Travel Queen camper. It saved our marriage – at least for a time.

Cathy too liked the camper. I thought so anyway. We didn't talk much about our likes or dislikes or about much of anything. We argued instead, yelled and screamed, sometimes in front of the kids. We were not happy, but still we liked going camping. In that tiny space the four of us nestled around the table, eating hot dogs and beans and drinking hot cocoa with marshmallows and pretended to be a happy family. Or maybe we really were happy – at least for those moments. It makes me sad now to think about it all.

Ever since I was a kid and my family spent part of each summer at the Jersey Shore, I've loved going to the beach. So I was eager to check out the Oregon coastal towns, hoping I would also find a refuge there. It was already late afternoon when we left on that first trip, Cathy poking around the kitchen, the girls reading books because we didn't let them watch TV till after dinner. When I announced, "Come on, we're driving to the Coast," the girls immediately screamed and cheered. Cathy didn't say anything. I couldn't tell whether she liked the idea. She was hard to read, though I didn't try very hard. I didn't know exactly where we were going. Someone at school had mentioned a place called Seaside, which sounded good, slightly New Jerseyish. Maybe they'd even have a boardwalk and some good restaurants or who knew what. Unfortunately, by the time we arrived on a foggy Sunday evening, it was already dark and the shops were all closing down. When we drove to the end of the main drag where there was a turnaround that ended at the beach, we couldn't even see the ocean, though when I rolled down the window we could hear the deep rumble of the breaking surf. I liked that, and took a deep breath of the salt air. I was glad, despite everything, that we were at the beach.

"This isn't any fun," Jessie said.

"Not everything has to be fun," I snapped, angry for no reason I could have said.

"We left too late," Cathy said. 'That's the problem."

"Thank you for the helpful advice." My jaw felt locked in place.

"I'm hungry," Gabrielle, the youngest, said.

"Okay, we can go get something to eat," I said. "There must be a good seafood place around somewhere."

"Somehow I doubt that," Cathy said. She slouched back against the passenger side door.

"Can't we walk on the beach," Jessie whined. "That's why we came all this way here."

"Can I have french fries, Daddy?" Gabe wanted to know.

"You don't need french fries," her mother told her. "You're already getting too chubby."

"Leave her alone," I said. "She's only seven years old for chrissake."

"That's when it all starts."

"You'd know, I guess," I said.

"What's that supposed to mean?" Cathy sat up straight and stared at me.

"Nothing," I mumbled. "Nothing at all."

I pulled the camper over to the side of the road. There were only a few people on the street, mostly old people walking tiny dogs. I kept the windshield wipers going and turned on the defroster.

"I don't think it's fair," Jessie said.

"What?" I said.

"That we drive all the way to here and then not get to go on the beach."

"It's dark, Jessie," I said. "You wouldn't even be able to see anything."

"Still, it's not fair."

"Shit," I said.

"Not in front of the kids," Cathy said.

I dropped my head on to the steering wheel. "Fine," I said and yanked up the emergency brake. "Everybody the fuck out. We're going for a walk on the beach."

"I don't think . . ." Cathy started to say, but I'd already opened the door and the kids were scrambling out behind me. "Put on your hats," I said.

"But I'm still hungry," Gay said again.

"Too bad," I said, feeling mean, "You'll just have to wait. We don't all get whatever we want whenever we want it."

Gabe started to cry then, a soft whimper that she tried to hide, which only made me feel like more of a shit. "Look sweetie," I put my arm around her little shoulder. "Later we can have french fries, and cheeseburgers too."

"You promise?"

"I promise."

"Come on," Jessie shouted. "This is gonna be fun." She was already running toward the sand and the ocean.

And she was right. It was fun. Even in the rain and cold. I guess that's what we had to learn about the Oregon Coast. It doesn't matter whether it's raining or sunny, or even if it's night or day. Or if you feel shitty and angry and upset and not so sure about the people you're with. You go anyway and make the best of it because no matter what the weather, or how you feel, the ocean is still there, and the waves are breaking, and the air is clean and smells of seaweeds and salt and damn if you're not closer after a long walk on the beach to what this damn life is supposed to be all about. That's what I think.

When He Died

I COULD TELL, EVEN though they didn't ask directly, that they wondered what I was doing there. I was wondering about that myself. All I knew was that it had been time for me to come see my father. Right away! And with that certainty, I had left work, said good-bye to my family, and bought a ticket on the earliest flight available.

My mother and father and brother all lived together in a condo complex in Cherry Hill, New Jersey, a place they moved to when my father retired from his medical practice. I think they saw it as a step up from the old family home in West Philadelphia – Mom thought it was very "modern." I found the place impersonal and depressing, but I kept that opinion to myself. If they were happy, fine. By moving to the other side of the country I had given up any right to speak about such decisions.

Dad had been going down hill steeply ever since his retirement. He'd quickly progressed from being forgetful, to repeating himself frequently, to wandering around the apartment in the middle of the night. It wasn't the first time I'd been witness to Dad's dementia, but it was clearly now even worse. Mom said, "Look, Meyer, who's come to see us? It's Butch." Though he smiled and shook my hand, I could tell he was having trouble figuring out who I was and why I was standing there. He looked frail, so unlike the strong man I had known as a child. When we were growing up, I rarely saw my father without a tie and jacket. He was a professional guy through and through. Now he was dressed in some sort of blue terry-cloth jumpsuit. I'm sure my mother had picked that out for him. When we went to sit down in the living room, Dad sat in his new chair, an uncomfortable looking Plexiglas affair, without even a place for him to put his feet up. He kept reaching toward a side table as if to pick something up. Then he would stop, not having found what he was searching for and bite his lip. "He wants to smoke," Mom whispered. "But the doctor says it's bad for him. So I had to take away all his stuff." Dad had been a cigar and pipe smoker his whole life. To this day, I can't think about him, without remembering the rummy smell of Prince Albert pipe tobacco.

"That doesn't seem right," I said. "I mean, what's it matter?"

"The doctor said," Mom insisted. "And anyway, I don't want that odor getting on all the new furniture." She looked around the room, nodding at each tacky, modern piece.

Our afternoon together was pleasant enough. We all settled into our roles in the family dynamic. Well, I guess Dad didn't remember his role. Else he wouldn't have been acting so darn friendly, even effusive in a rambling sort of way. This was very much unlike the way he'd always behaved – reserved, dignified to a fault, often silent, sometimes terribly angry, especially when he imagined he was being disrespected. Now he was telling me a story about his college days at the University of Pennsylvania, when he went to eat in the college commissary, whose name (Houston Hall) he remarkably remembered. "They didn't have anything to eat I even recognized. It was all *treyf*. Covered in gravy. I just pointed at stuff. The workers must have thought I came from the old country, a greenhorn." He laughed. "That's the way I felt, Butchie." He reached over and patted my knee.

I was dumbstruck. It had been many years, since my father had called me by my childhood nickname, and even longer since he'd reached out to touch me in any way other than a manly handshake. This was the man I'd always wanted for my father, the one who maybe had always been there, hiding. He even asked me about my family and my work and then really paid attention to my answers.

Mom made dinner for us that evening, a special effort for her I was made to understand. "Usually we order in," she told me. "Or we send Paul to the deli."

"Well, I appreciate it," I said, as I chewed a mouthful of dry meatloaf. My mother had never been a good cook. "Maybe tomorrow night I can take you all out for dinner. We can go some place nice."

"I don't think we can do that," Mom said. "Your father," she nodded in Dad's direction at the head of the table as if I maybe didn't know who he was," "He doesn't do so well out in public anymore."

"What do you mean?"

"Sometimes he spills. Or the food's too tough for him."

"So we order something soft. I'm sure he's not the only person in the world who can't chew so well anymore."

Dad just kept eating as if the subject under discussion was of no interest to him. I began to suspect that maybe Dad wasn't as far gone as he put on. Maybe he was dropping out, going inside, much like I'd done when I was sixteen.

"Fine," I said, "Well, then I'll make dinner tomorrow night for us all."

"We could get pizza," Paul said.

"Or Chinese," Mom said.

Dad finally tuned in. "Let the boy make the dinner," he said. "Who knew he could even cook."

That evening we all watched TV, nobody had much to say; we settled into our standard silence until it was time to go to bed. Ten o'clock for Mom and Dad; Paul soon thereafter. "Want to drive down the Shore tomorrow?" I asked him, before he went off.

"I'm still working," he said. "It's just a regular day for me."

"Okay," I said, "goodnight."

I stayed up to watch Letterman, then fell into a restless sleep on the living room couch. Some hours later, Mom's voice woke me up. "He can't breathe," she was saying.

"Huh?" I was struggling to figure out where I was.

"Your father stopped breathing. He's in the bedroom." She pointed. "Go in there. Please."

I ran into their bedroom, Mom stayed out in the living room. Dad was lying on his back in the bed, wearing only his underwear. All the blankets were on the floor. I could hear him struggling to breathe, a rasping noise in his throat and chest. I went up to the side of the bed and grabbed his hand. He didn't respond to me. The wheezing and rasping noise continued, like a broken engine. Only later was I to realize that this was what people called the "death rattle."

Just then Paul came rushing into the room. "What's going on?" He was dressed only in his underwear also. I could almost imagine the whole thing was a dream. But it wasn't.

"He can't get his breath. Listen."

"I'll go call 911," Paul said.

"I'm not so sure that'll help." I knew Dad was not going to last much longer.

"Still, I better call," he said. "You okay here?"

"I'm okay."

Then I was alone with my dying father. I wanted to say something to him, but nothing came to mind. And I didn't think he could hear me anyhow. Finally, I bent over and kissed his forehead, and left my lips there. It seemed to calm him. The rasping became slower, then died away completely. I listened for any breath at all, and there was none. I don't know how long the whole process had taken, maybe minutes, maybe much longer, but I held him until the medics, summoned by my brother, came storming into the room, stretcher and medical paraphernalia in hand. They rushed over and grabbed hold of Dad, ready to pull him off the bed and begin administering CPR, or whatever it is that's done in these situations, but I came to my senses, and yelled, "Stop. Leave him alone."

"Who are you?" the lead medic said.

"I'm his son." I was still the only family member in the room.

"And you're sure that's what he would want."

"I'm sure," I said. And I was, without having to think about it. They packed up their stuff and left. I pulled a sheet up over Dad, not over his face, kissed him once again, and went out to talk to my mother.

She was still sitting in the living room, a robe pulled around her shoulders. I sat down next to her, and took her hand. "He's gone," I said. Then I started to cry. I needed some relief.

"Don't you do that," Mom said. "If you start crying, then I will too."

I made myself stop, though it was hard to do. "Okay. It's okay, Mom."

Paul walked in then, phone in hand. "I called the funeral home. They'll be here soon to pick up the body."

"Don't you want to go see him before they get here?" I asked them both. But Mom just shook her head, and Paul walked into the kitchen.

IT WASN'T TILL MANY months later, back in Portland, that I was finally able to cry. I don't even know what precipitated it, but one minute I was starting to make dinner for the family, and the next I was on my knees, wracked with sobs. I hadn't cried like that since I was a small boy. Something broke open inside me.

When my wife got home later that evening, I pulled her aside. The kids were running in and out of the kitchen, asking what was for dinner. "You know, I really did love my Dad," I told her. I thought I might start to cry again.

She put a hand on my shoulder. "I know you did, honey," she said. "That's why you went back."

The Day They Shot Our Dog

The move to the country would be healthier for the kids, we reasoned, and maybe better for our struggling marriage. I'd always been a city boy; spent the majority of my adult life in urban settings, the previous seven years in Seattle. Little did I know what real rural life was like.

I had accepted a teaching job at a high school, about 30 miles west of Portland. The town seemed pleasant enough. Lots of trees and farmland, if you liked that sort of thing. Cathy seemed to. She was originally a small town girl and never looked fully comfortable with our urban lifestyle and hippy-dippy friends. I think for her moving to rural Oregon was a relief.

We settled in and began a new life out at the end of Jack Road, up a steep gravel driveway. Cathy took a job as a landscaper's helper, a hands-on physical job, but she liked the work, coming home every night with a smile on her face and dirt caked under her fingernails. She looked good too, healthy and flushed from the sun.

We tried to adjust to rural life. Some of it was quite lovely. The rented house sat on ten acres of wooded property. Jessie, most of all, would wander off for hours, alone among the trees. I was later to learn that she was having a hard time with the socialization process in 6th grade. One Saturday afternoon I took her to the mall in Hillsboro, the closest sizable town, to buy some new school clothes. On our way out of one of the chain brand stores, we saw a guy with a box of puppies. Jessie wanted to look. Mixed brown mongrels jumped, desperate to be held, in their own animal way knowing this was the only chance they had. Jessie was immediately in love. Maybe it would be good for all of us to have a pet, I thought. Somewhere I remembered that Cathy was not fond of dogs. I conveniently put that out of my head and watched as Jessie picked the puppy she wanted, the one that most assiduously licked her face. I paid the dog guy the ten dollars he was asking. On the drive home, we named the pup Chinook, a male, who looked to have some German Shepherd in its genes.

I'll never forget the expression on C's face when we arrived home with the mutt. Her look said it all; said this adds another stick to the load I'm already tired of carrying. Said, you bastard, I can't take the dog away from our daughter, but I'd like to, would like to take it and you out to the creek and drown you both. She picked up the puppy in the box and went with Jessie and now an excited Gabrielle to make a space for the dog in the garage. Didn't say a word to me.

The dog thrived, became a loved member of the family, but was not well trained or disciplined. We all made halfhearted efforts, but it was easier to simply let Chinook roam about. If he was getting into mischief, well, that's what country dogs did. Only problem was that we did have neighbors out in the boonies. The Dobers lived on the spread adjacent to ours. They had three teenaged boys, who trapped animals and sold their pelts. I'd only spoken a few words to Jed Dober, the patriarch, a stocky, grizzled looking man, a guy who worked his whole life with his hands, and was thus, both admirable and unknowable to me. My dad didn't even own a hammer.

The Dobers had a flock of ducks and chickens on their property, which extended down the driveway to an algae covered pond where the ducks paddled about. Some days we would hear Chinook barking at the birds, but didn't think too much about it. He was still a puppy, still harmless.

Dober walked over to our house one afternoon to tell me that our pup was threatening the ducks, not just barking, but chasing and snapping, and, in his words, "It can't happen no more."

"But your dogs are down there too. " I pointed at his two brutish looking dogs, snuffling the dirt not twenty yards in front of us.

"My dogs don't chase livestock," Dober said. "I'd have the boys put them down if they did." He pulled his billed wool hat further down over his forehead.

"What do you mean by that?" I asked.

"Keep your dog away from the pond."

At dinner, I told the girls they should keep a better eye on Chinook and not let him wander about so much.

"Maybe you should get home and take him for a walk then," Cathy said. "We can't leave him locked up all day with no exercise."

"I have a job," I snapped at her. "In case you hadn't noticed."

"And you're the one who brought that dog in here, in case you hadn't noticed."

"Chinook belongs to everyone," I said. "You don't want me to get rid of him, do you?"

She stared at her dinner plate.

There was no doubt that the girls really loved this big gangly puppy, even though they were not so good at taking care of him. There were piles of dog shit all over the property.

"I'll walk him," Gay said, "As soon as I get home from school."

"You're too small," Jessie said. "Chinook will pull you all over the place."

"Not if I talk to him nice," Gay insisted. "He listens to me."

"Oh yeah," Jesse said. "You talk dog language I guess."

"You'll both walk him," I interrupted. "If you want to have a dog, you have to take responsibility." I glanced over at Cathy, hoping she was appreciating my display of good parenting. "And use that leash I bought. Don't just let him run amok."

"What's a muck?" Gay asked.

"Just use the leash," I said. We all laughed. And so that was settled.

I didn't hear from Dober again. The girls were

keeping up their end of the bargain, at least that's what they were telling me. Since I was keeping long hours at the high school, I didn't get home till well after the girls and Cathy did.

It was while we were all sitting down to dinner, around 6:30, that we heard the shot. It was very loud, like a car backfiring, but a few seconds after the blast we all heard the wail, a high-pitched squeal, that we knew immediately was Chinook. I pushed away from the table and ran out the front door, the rest of the family following behind. On one side of the dirt road, next to the pond, lay our dog, keeled over on his side, his tongue hanging out. The girls ran over and stooped beside their pet. On the other side of the road, stood one of the older Dober boys, cradling in his arms a long shotgun.

"Chinook has a hole in his side, Daddy," Jessie screamed. Gay was already sobbing.

"What the hell is going on here?" I demanded of the boy. "Did you shoot that dog?"

"My dad said not to let him bother the ducks no more. He was down here every day. Killed two of them." He looked down at the dirt and scuffed his foot around. "I'm sorry, I didn't mean to hurt him."

"You didn't mean to hurt him? What the fuck did you think would happen when you fired a goddamned gun."

I knelt down by the girls and Cathy. Chinook had a gaping hole in his side.

"Is Chinook going to die?" Jessie asked.

"I don't know," I lied. "Let's get him up to the house." I shoved my hands underneath the warm body and lifted up. Blood spilled on to the sleeves of my shirt. Cathy took the girls by the hand and they followed me back up the driveway. As we passed the Dobers' place, Jed Dober stood there with his arms crossed over his chest. "Didn't mean for him to shoot the dog," he said. "Just wanted to warn you."

I stopped and stared at him, the dog sagging in my arms, the girls crying behind me. I couldn't find any words. I turned away and hurried up to our front yard. I imagined a racing trip into town, to an animal hospital if we could find one, but Chinook had taken his last breath by the time I laid him down at our doorstep.

We buried him that evening, out behind the vegetable garden and the sunflowers that Cathy had planted. We put his leash in there with him and his favorite toys and Cathy said a prayer and each of the girls said good-bye and I shoveled dirt into the grave until it was mounded up on top.

"Do dogs go to heaven?" Gabrielle asked.

"I don't know," I told her. "Maybe."

"Chinook should go to heaven," she said. "Even if he did eat that duck."

"Yeah, sweetie," I said. "I bet he will."

BEFORE THE NEXT SCHOOL year started, we moved out of Banks, into the next town down the road. None of us had been able to recover from Chinook's death. All the beauty and freedom felt sucked out of that country landscape. Now it was full of danger and pain and even death. City kids don't know about all the dying. We like to make up that hamburger only exists as a product under cellophane. The Dober family had no such conceits. They depended on the yearly deer or elk for their meat supply. Some days after the shooting the youngest son brought over a hunk of venison for us. I don't know if it was a peace offering or a simple neighborly gesture, but I accepted the meat and cooked it that night. The girls refused to try it.

Out in the country a dog getting shot is no big deal. Especially one that is young and crazy and chases after the neighbors' ducks. But to our little family it was the end of a promise. Jessie has claimed not to like dogs ever since that day. She has yet to own another pet. Gabrielle and I still talk about what happened, a marker in our lives: the trip to Maui, graduation day, the divorce, when Chinook got shot.

For my part, I still have questions. Why didn't I rip the gun away and throw it in the pond, scream at old man Dober, set poison out for his dogs? The truth, though? It all comes back on me. Everything would have been different if I had taken the time to train that dog properly, if I hadn't bought it without talking to my wife. If I hadn't gone where I didn't belong.

Part Five

Getting On, Getting Old

Father and Daughter

"I've got a new girlfriend, Dad," Gabrielle told me. We were speaking on the phone, which we did almost every evening, catching each other up on the day's events.

"Good," I said, "Can't have too many friends."

"No," Gay said, "I mean, like a *girlfriend*, girlfriend."

"Huh?"

"Don't be dense, Dad." Gabrielle sighed.

"It's my natural state," I said, still trying to figure out what we were talking about.

"Her name is Jaelynne. She's from Texas. I met her when I was out dancing at The Wildrose."

"The Wildrose?"

"It's a gay bar."

"Oh," I said quietly.

"Damn, do I have to come out to you again?" It was hard to tell whether she was amused or exasperated.

"When was the first time?"

"Jesus, Dad. I told you before. I said I liked girls better than boys."

"Who doesn't. But I didn't think that meant, you know. What you're saying."

"It's okay to say the word, Dad."

"What word?"

"Lesbian."

Gabrielle is my younger daughter, nineteen at the time of this call. She'd dropped out of her first year at Evergreen State College. She said she was unhappy and came to live in Seattle with me and my new girlfriend, Judy. After a month with us, during which time her hair color changed four times and her depression lifted, Gabrielle found an apartment of her own.

I'd always felt like we were more than father and daughter. After her mother and I got divorced, Gay, who was then in high school, lived most of the time with me. We went everywhere together, often holding hands as we strolled through our Hawthorne neighborhood. I bragged to Judy about how I could talk to Gay about anything. "That's not always such a good idea," she said, which puzzled me. But I didn't pursue it. Judy was a naturopath, a "healer" she called herself; all sort of woo-woo, I thought. She ate raw garlic, and was always analyzing me, which drove me even more crazy that I was already feeling. "She's your daughter, not your friend," Judy said, and stared at me knowingly.

"You mean you're gay?" I asked, and when there was no answer to that, said, "That's sort of funny, isn't it?"

"How so?" Gabrielle sounded impatient.

"Well, you know, that's your nickname and all. Gay."

"You're the only one who calls me that."

"No," I insisted, "Your friends do too."

"Not since third grade, Dad."

"Really?"

"Really."

I took a deep breath and told myself to stop acting like an idiot. Then asked, "So, are you sure you really don't like boys?"

There was silence at the other end of the line; I stumbled on. "I mean, maybe you just haven't met the right guy. You don't really have a lot of experience. There are all sorts of nice boys out there."

"I thought you'd be cooler about this," Gabrielle said.

"Well, it's a bit of a shock is all." I took another breath and tried to redeem myself. "So, when do I get to meet this girlfriend, this *Jaelynne*."

"I don't know, Dad. Maybe not right now. I think I need some space."

Feeling wretched, wanting to start over, I said, "I can give you space, sweetie."

"Let's talk later," she said.

"Maybe we can meet for coffee tomorrow."

"I'll call you when I'm ready," Gabrielle said.

"I think being gay is just fine," I blurted. "Really."

"See ya, Dad," Gabrielle said and hung up the phone.

Things between Gabrielle and I changed after that. It wasn't about the phone call or her new girlfriend, or mine, or any of that. There just comes a time when a father and a daughter need to move further apart. It was damn hard for me – fucking agony to tell the truth. I did not want to let go. Gabrielle had to hold firm till she was ready. And she did.

My Cars, My Life

I've had a bunch of them – all kinds of colors and body types. Cars, that is, automobiles. I can almost measure my life by the vehicles I've owned.

The first was a 1954 Buick Special – two-tone gray and white, a hand me down from my father, and the car I learned to drive in. My mother taught me – sort of. I mean she didn't seem to be paying a lot of attention during our lessons. She mostly smoked cigarettes and looked out the window. Once when I went straight through a stop sign, she didn't even notice.

Near the end of my senior year in college, I talked my dad into putting up the money for my first brand new car. I told him I would start paying him back when I graduated. I never did re-pay the full amount, which I still feel guilty about. Dad went with me to visit the auto showrooms. It was different back then, in 1966. There were fewer choices in cars, mostly all American-made, Fords and Chevys and even ugly Studebakers, but I was attracted to the new Volkswagen dealership. The tiny cars seemed almost like toys, compared to the big Pontiac and Oldsmobile cruisers Dad and I test drove. I didn't think then about the implications of a Jewish guy buying a car from a company that supported the Nazis; neither did my dad say anything about it, which I still wonder about. I ended up buying a dark green Beetle, with a sliding sunroof. Paid $1300 dollars – or rather Dad did. I loved everything about that car – the smell, the tinny little radio, the way it tried so hard to get up to speed on the highway. I mean, I loved it for all its faults, not despite them. I felt the car was right for me.

Unfortunately, that first summer after graduation, I was driving in the rain – too fast – hit a skid on the Long Beach Island Causeway, and spun halfway through a guard rail that stopped me from plunging a thousand feet down into Barnegat Bay. While the car careened, I remember thinking that I was about to die, which surprisingly filled me with a sort of inner peace. I survived, unhurt, but the little Bug was never the same.

After that I didn't have the heart (or money) to purchase another new car and settled for a series of $500 junkers. Most served me about as well as I thought they would. Some were even pretty cool to own – like the black 1949 Ford that I bought for $75 before anybody realized that such cars were "classics."

After I got married and my wife and I had our first child and decided that we wanted to move out west – hippies that we were – we got our limited cash together and bought a bright red 1972 Dodge pick-up. And I set to work building a camper home on the back for our cross-country voyage. I wonder now how we had such blind optimism, or why we weren't more scared. Maybe that's just the nature of being young. The camper was way over-built. I used 2x4's and ¾ inch plywood, the rear of the truck sagged, but it was cozy inside. I built bunks with storage space underneath and found an old camper stove. We felt like pioneers, traveling across the breadth of the country, stopping to camp by the side of the road or along a riverbank, waking up in a new place every day. It was all a great adventure. Our life was as expansive as the endless vistas of the country.

When our second child, Gabrielle, was born, we graduated to a full-blown recreational vehicle – an old one to be sure, but a damn beauty. Bought it from a friend for $1,000 – the best deal of my life. It was a 1969 International ¾ ton pick-up with a Travel Queen camper mounted on the bed. Though old, it had been treated very well by the previous owner – my friend's dad. It had all the bells and whistles I wanted, foldout bunks, a full kitchenette with an oven, a sink and a propane furnace, and, best of all, an extension over the cab of the truck which served as a bed and hideout for Gabe and Jessie. The rig even had an intercom system so the girls could talk to us from their bunk while we were driving down the highway. That would be considered illegal these days, but we weren't concerned then. The girls loved their little hideaway. They still talk about it. We went camping almost every weekend and holiday when we had the Travel Queen. I was teaching during the week, but free once Friday came around. For a time, that vehicle saved our marriage. We didn't seem to fight as much when we were on the road. It wasn't just escapism, though that played a part. But in the camper, we had a shared purpose and destination; we worked together well, something we failed at miserably in our stationary environment. Maybe we should have just kept traveling – on the road, all the time. It's a thought.

As the kids grew older and developed their own sets of friends, they had less and less interest in taking camping trips with Mom and Dad, and so we eventually sold the beautiful Travel Queen. I still miss it. Funny how you can come to be so fond of a hunk of steel. I still sometimes dream about driving down a lonely highway in that truck.

In mid-life, when I was a proper citizen and working hard each day to support my family and mostly forgetting about my youthful dreams and aspirations, I had boring cars. Just whatever would get me back and forth to work and look presentable. My cars had to be dependable – that was the key word. That was my life then. The cars themselves are barely rememberable – a yellow Volvo, a Ford Focus, a Volkswagen Fox, blah, blah, fucking blah.

And then after 22 years, my wife and I decided we'd had enough. I think we both were scared, but breathed a sigh of relief, and went our separate ways. I gave Cathy whatever car we had at the time. I truthfully don't even remember what it was. Then I went out and bought another pick-up, one with a shell camper, just big enough for one. It was time to start over.

Forbidden Fruit

I knew it was the wrong thing to do. Well, maybe not at first. But then it just snuck up on me, and by that time I was too far gone to make a decent decision. That's what happened with me and Mimi.

We were doing a play together, and you know how those things go. The actors become unusually close – intimate, sharing dressing rooms and reaching deep into their souls to find connection on stage – and sometimes off. I'd been single for some years then, after my first marriage went to dust, so relished the occasional intimacy.

One day after rehearsal, only Mimi and I were left in the theater, still running lines, when Mimi put down her script and stepped up close to me. "You know, I'm really attracted to you," she said.

Her whispered words really surprised me. "But I, uh, thought you were married," I stuttered.

She smiled at me in a way that was both seductive and sad. I only then fully recognized what an attractive woman she was – dark-haired and intense. "It doesn't matter," she said. "Not to me."

I was both flattered and confused. Flattery won out. "So what do we do now?" I asked.

Mimi moved closer. That's when we kissed.

As the weeks and months went by, our flirtation blossomed into a full-blown romance, with all the joy and pain associated with such things. Well, maybe not all. We weren't sleeping together. Mimi felt that if she held back on this last step, she was, in some way, still being faithful to her marriage. I think we were both feeling uneasy, even scared about what was happening. But we were also in love or some semblance of it. And neither of us knew what to do. Frankly, I was not sure I wanted to do anything other than enjoy the moments. My experiences with relationships up to that point were not stellar. I had married right out of college to a woman who I quickly discovered I had nothing in common with – including intellectual interests and religion. Two biggies. But with Mimi we connected on almost every level. Like me, she was Jewish, and we both had recently come back to our roots in the religion. A spiritual path that I had rejected for many years – out of cynicism and dissatisfaction with my own life, suddenly seemed full of hope – and joy. Then there was the whole artist thing. I was a writer. So was Mimi. I had recently developed an interest in performing, as had Mimi. We had the same sense of humor. Could talk for hours. And the more we had to withhold, the deeper our physical attraction grew. I know it sounds sappy, but I truly believed I had finally found my soul mate. "It's *bashert*," Mimi said. The Hebrew word for fate. I didn't disagree.

The play went well. And after, Mimi and I decided to work together again on a new production that we would write ourselves. We even already had a name for it: *The Two-Headed Person.* We were meeting and rehearsing every day. I'd never felt more artistically stimulated. And after rehearsals it was hard to keep our hands off of each other. It would have been perfect. Except for the overriding reality of Mimi's marriage. She had a husband at home. And a young daughter. The whole situation was untenable, maybe even immoral. I tried to convince her to leave her husband, Henry, a college physics professor. "Better now than later," I said. "Clearly you don't love him."

Mimi looked stricken. "I can't do that," she said. "We made promises."

"What do you mean?" I asked.

"It's not something I can talk about. But I couldn't do that to Henry. I just couldn't." She started to cry.

I knew the situation couldn't continue. At least not like it was, and pretty soon Henry figured out what was going on. He called me on the phone. The whole thing felt surreal. He didn't even seem all that angry. Instead his voice sounded reasonable. It didn't fit with the picture of him as an abusive and demanding guy that Mimi had been painting for me. "Look," Henry said, "I can understand how these things happen. But I'd really appreciate it if you would stop now. I mean, enough is enough, right?" I think he may have even chuckled.

"Well, I think that you need to talk to Mimi about all this."

"Yes, definitely," he said. "We've obviously got a lot of work to do."

Now I really felt sorry for the guy. I didn't know what to say. I almost felt like consoling him. "Yeah, well, maybe I can talk to her also. See where we all stand."

"I'd appreciate that. I really would," Henry said. I thought I heard a break in his voice.

When I told Mimi about the call, she was furious. "Goddamn him," she hissed. "Goddamn him to hell." I was surprised by her vehemence.

"Look, maybe we all have to take a step back," I said.

"Is that what you really want?" Mimi moved in close and put a hand on my chest.

"I wish we had met earlier," I said, feeling lame. "I should have fallen in love with you when I was 25."

"Me too, but that's not what we've got."

"So, you tell me. What do you want to do? I think you've got to choose. Henry or me?"

"I just don't know," she said, and began, not for the first time, to cry. "It's too hard."

"Tell you what," I said. "Let's do the show, put all our energy into that, then make a decision."

"Okay," she quickly agreed. I think we were both relieved to be able to put the dilemma aside for a time. I know I was, but I also knew somewhere, not so deep down, that what I was doing was wrong, was hurtful, and just plain stupid. If we continued on, it wouldn't turn out well for any of us.

After the run of our somewhat self-indulgent show

(which Henry attended – and even applauded heartily) it was time to have the big talk. Mimi and I walked over to a local bar that was frequented by older gay men, a peaceful kind of place. I think we both knew what was coming. "I'm going to return to my family," Mimi said, watching my reaction over the rim of her wine glass."

"Yeah, probably for the best," I said.

"So you're okay with it?" she asked.

"No," I said. "Not okay. I feel shitty. But, it is what it is."

"I hate that phrase," Mimi said. "What does it even mean?"

"Forget it. I was just trying to say that I think you're making the right decision. I wouldn't have had the guts to do it on my own."

"You sound like you're relieved."

"Maybe I am." I stared down at the table. "We can still be friends."

"God, you're full of clichés today." She seemed almost angry. I think it was her way to get through this.

"Sorry."

"Don't be." Then her demeanor softened. "I'm the one who should be sorry. Look what I've put you through."

"I've been a willing participant." We both smiled.

"It was a good show, wasn't it?" Mimi said.

"Yeah, it was," I replied. "It was lovely."

She got up then, leaned over and kissed me on the cheek. "See you around?"

"Yeah," I said. "See you around."

We did see each other "around" for a while, but when we did it always felt awkward. We spoke enough for Mimi to tell me that her marriage was doing okay; she and Henry were seeing a couples therapist. I told her I was happy for her. I later started dating another (single) woman, also Jewish, beautiful, and smart. We later married.

So maybe it all wasn't really *bashert* with Mimi and me. And maybe it was, but who were we to try and understand how fate truly works.

A Jew in a Catholic School

"What's a Jewish guy doing teaching in a Catholic school?" My mother wasn't the first one to be puzzled by my current employment, though perhaps the frankest. Others massaged the point, as in, "So what's it like for you at that place?" or "Don't you feel uncomfortable there?"

I answered all with a noncommittal shrug. "It's no big deal," I said. Which is what I believed – at first.

I had needed a job after a series of budget cuts at the public high school where I taught put my position, as one of the newer teachers, in jeopardy. So, when I heard about the opening for an English teacher at Ignatius High School I didn't hesitate to send in my resume.

No one mentioned Catholicism at the interview. Nor did anyone broach the subject of my Jewishness; though there was a line on the application that asked about religious preference. I had printed in all caps, JEWISH. No sense in messing around.

But even the Jesuit priest who was part of the interview panel wanted only to know how I would teach "Moby Dick" to a classroom full of antsy boys. "I'll take them out on the ocean," I answered. "Step by step, so they don't get seasick." The priest looked at me quizzically, but I thought I saw the beginning of a grin.

There were lots of questions about classroom discipline. They seemed to be most interested in my ability to keep order. Apparently, in an all-boys school this could be a major issue. I guess my answers or my experience must have satisfied them because at the end of the interview the school principal turned to me and said, "Okay, the job is yours if you want it."

"Absolutely," I told him, and shook hands all around. It was only as I was leaving the building and passed under the gilded plaster statue of Jesus Christ nailed on the cross that I stopped, looked up, and muttered, "Man, what the hell are you doing?"

They were right about the classroom discipline thing. Turns out there is something in an all-boys classroom that moves it toward both rowdiness and testing. They will push you as far and as hard as you allow yourself to be moved. On the other hand, once you stand up to their pretend thuggishness, stare them down, and lay out the consequences for boorish behavior, those same boys will become your best pals. The boys at Ignatius were not a bad lot. Far from it. They were all college bound, many to the top schools in the country. Accustomed to public school classrooms in Philadelphia, Seattle, and rural Oregon I was startled when I gave my first homework assignment and watched all twenty-five students take out their notebooks and copy down my instructions, even asking questions for clarification. I was even more flabbergasted on the following day when every one of those young men presented me with a completed assignment, most of them typed. Yes, indeed, I thought. I'm going to like it here.

And I did. I was able to teach at a higher level than I had previously, and I no longer had to worry about keeping the material accessible to that imagined lowest common denominator. They liked both "Moby Dick" and "The Great Gatsby," though after a grueling three month line-by-line explication of the former, my senior honors class had a ritual burning of their paper back copies of Ahab and the white whale. They told me all about it, grinning like fools. And I too laughed at their literary desecration. "At least you'll never forget old Melville," I said. "Or old Mr. Freedman," one of the boys responded.

My first comeuppance occurred during the student mass held every Friday morning. Attendance mandatory, Catholic or not. I'd never been to a mass before and felt a nervous knot building in my gut as I walked with my neatly dressed boys to the school chapel. Everyone was on his best behavior. I was struck by the absence of all the usual joking, gabbing, and roughhousing. Father Robins, the most fearsome of the Jesuits, stood at the entrance with his bare arms crossed, his expression a mask of Christian hostility. I had already heard stories of Father Robins taking misbehaving students into the restroom and delivering some Old Testament retribution.

The service itself was not so bad. I followed along with the readings and listened to the sermon. It was a lot like synagogue services: well-intentioned, moral, and a bit boring. I heard no comments about killers of Christ, though I was bracing for them. Things only went awry when it was time for communion. I had a vague idea of what this ritual entailed. It had always struck me a bit weird. Drinking the blood of the savior? But here now in its presence, I was more curious than put off. Indeed, as each row of boys rose to move to the front of the chapel, I felt more and more drawn to the drama of it all: the angelic smiles on the faces of the boys as they opened their mouths like baby birds and waited for that opaque disc, the way complete silence prevailed except for the muttering of the priests, the strangely fussy way the rim of the wine cup was wiped with a cloth after each communicant took his sip. When it came time for our row to stand and move to the front, I felt like I could do little else except go with them.

Father Olive was dispensing the wafers for our line. He was a fat, red-cheeked man of indeterminate age. The boys, I knew, sarcastically called him Jolly Ollie. When I reached the front of the line, I held my hands cupped in front of me, mimicking those who preferred receiving the wafer in their hands. No way I wanted the priest's pudgy fingers in my mouth. But Father Olive seemed stuck, looking at me like he'd bitten into a rotten peach. I nodded at him and smiled. There was another long moment of hesitation. Then he frowned and placed the wafer in my palms. I popped it in my mouth and chewed. It was fairly tasteless, like matzo that has gone soft. "Yum," I said. Father Ollie looked horrified. I felt slightly puzzled as I went and received my wine and returned to my seat.

The following Monday I received a message that the president of the school wanted to see me in his office. Though I have a lifelong antipathy toward authority figures, I wasn't overly concerned. Father William Nehri was in charge of both the religious order and the school. I had yet to meet the man. Maybe he simply wanted to welcome me to the community.

We shook hands and Father Nehri indicated I should take a seat in the heavy wood chair opposite his wide desk. He was a serious looking fellow, thin lipped with gray hair cut close to the scalp, military style. "So, how are you settling into life here at Ignatius?" He smiled crookedly.

"So far, so good."

"Somewhat different from the public schools, isn't it?"

"Kids are kids," I said.

"Indeed." Father Nehri sat forward and clasped his hands. Apparently I was expected to continue.

"Well, I will admit that having all boys in the classroom is a big change."

"We find that our students learn best in a single gender environment."

"Could be," I said, but wondered how they tested that theory.

"Our parents expect very positive results when they entrust their boys to us."

"That makes sense," I said, not knowing quite where we were headed.

Without further preliminaries, the priest said, "I understand you practice Judaism." He stared at me like he expected a Star of David to appear on my forehead.

"Well, I don't need to practice that much," I said. "I'm already pretty good at it."

Father Nehri didn't laugh. "You do understand how important providing a strong Catholic faith is to our educational process?"

Now it was my turn to sit forward. "Are you asking me whether being Jewish gets in the way of my teaching?"

"No. We have had to accommodate ourselves to having a number of secular teachers here." His voice became stern. "What I cannot and will not accept is any mockery of the sacred."

"I would never do that. I don't go around mocking anyone's religion and I expect them not to mock mine."

"Mr. Freedman, do you understand the significance of Holy Communion?"

I slumped back. So that was it. "Not entirely," I said. "I know what it represents."

"It is our most sacred ritual, a portrayal of the ultimate sacrifice of our Lord, and it is not, I repeat, not, for those who have yet to accept Jesus Christ as their savior."

"This is about my getting the wafer then," I said quietly. "I thought that's what I was supposed to do."

"You put Father Olive in a very difficult position. Only practicing Catholics may receive the Eucharist."

"No body and blood for me, huh?"

"This is nothing to joke about."

I felt a flush of heat rising into my cheeks. I didn't like being lectured to and I did not like being told I could not do something because I was Jewish. "The whole business seems a bit barbaric to me anyway," I blurted out.

"What?" Father William was clearly astonished.

"I mean, I get that Jesus was a great guy and all, but why pretend to eat his body and drink his blood? It seems strange."

Nehri stood up quickly, so I did too. "I do not care one whit about your opinions," he fumed. "You are never to take communion again. Is that understood?"

"Does that mean I don't have to go to mass anymore?"

"You have to do what every other teacher does." His hands were clenched at his sides, the skin of his neck was mottled red above his tight white collar.

"So what do I do when everybody goes up to get their wine and bread?"

"You stay in your seat, or else you may walk up and cross your hands one over the other. Like this." He demonstrated the position. "Then we can bless you as an outsider, without your receiving the holy wafer."

"I guess I'll stay on the bench then. Every team needs a benchwarmer, huh?"

"I think we're finished here." He looked at his watch, a heavy gold one. "I hope you will take our little talk to heart and that we will not have a need for further meetings."

I remembered that I wanted to keep this job and that I had a family that enjoyed eating regularly, so I said, "I'll try to be more respectful of the, uh, situation here."

"Good," he said. "That's all I ask."

I reached out my hand and we shook, though neither of our grips was particularly firm.

As I walked back to my classroom, a sense of despair perched on my shoulders. I thought, man, you screwed up again. I remembered the line from an old Bob Dylan song, something about how, "One should never go where one does not belong." It hit me like a punch in the gut. I took a deep breath, even thought about walking out the front door and never coming back, but then I stopped. Screw it, I told myself, just go back to your classroom and teach. That's all you're supposed to do. Which is exactly what I did. Stayed at that school for many years and nobody ever bothered me again about being Jewish. I was even invited into some of the religion classes to talk about Judaism. I made close friends with one of the Jesuit Brothers and even would drink coffee and talk baseball with Father Robins.

So, I don't know if Dylan was right or wrong about that belonging thing. What I would say if I was writing the song is: sometimes one can go where one does not belong, and one can learn to like it there, as long as they respect the rules. But I guess that would make for a lousy lyric. Wouldn't sound good with a harmonica at all.

Jew Bunny – Part 3

Part of the impetus for my return to Judaism was my divorce. I had stayed married to Catherine, a non-Jewish woman for 20 years, and despite our many differences, did manage to lovingly raise two wonderful daughters. Neither of the girls received much in the way of religious training. My wife and I initially agreed, without much discussion, to avoid any religious or spiritual training or indoctrination. Cathy, as the years went by, however, moved back into a close relationship with a form of fundamentalist Christianity. I found this hard to countenance, especially when on one trip to visit my parents at their Jersey Shore summer cottage, my gentile wife asked my mother if she was worried about "where your soul will go after you die if you don't accept Jesus as your lord." Mom was sputteringly angry when she told me about this, and I was likewise incensed. Why I didn't run for the hills at that point, I don't know. Instead, I consciously decided not to think about my situation. We were staying together for the kids, I told myself. But that wasn't all of it certainly. I had settled into feeling old and hopeless way before my time. It wasn't good for me, or for Cathy, and certainly not for the girls.

After that summer trip, and one of our most fearsome arguments, Cathy agreed not to proselytize, and not to take the girls to church with her. And I settled back into making a living and focusing on my daughters. We would light candles on Hanukah and have a tree with all the decorations on Christmas. Not very deep down, I felt besmirched by that tree. It brought back memories of being asked to sing Christmas carols in elementary school, and the intense feeling of shame that these carols engendered. Mom told me, when I confessed how upset I was, that I should sing the songs anyway, but silently mouth the word "Jesus" every time we came to it. I still felt awful. How had I now bought into experiencing this same moral confusion on a daily basis? Walking around, silently mouthing the words to my life.

After the divorce, I knew I had work to do on myself, though a return to Judaism was still far from my thoughts. And, after a few months, when I tentatively waded back into the dating pool, it was not Jewish women that I was looking for or attracted to. Jewish women were scary. My core anti-Semitic feelings were still in play. Jewish women were too bossy, too pushy, not even pretty. I was still seeing the world partially through my mother's eyes.

But now something else began to form in my muddled brain. I began to recognize that there had to be something else to live for, something greater than my own neurotic needs. And that something greater could not be embodied in a relationship with another person, at least not until I could bring to that relationship myself – with a sense of my own identity, my weaknesses and strengths, and my history. Otherwise, I would remain forever damaged and needy and useless to everybody. After an aborted, though interesting, foray into Buddhism, it occurred to me that maybe I needed to get back to my own religious roots. Or at least, give it a proper shot. I began checking out the local synagogues.

I signed up for classes in Judaism at a Conservative Temple in Mercer Island, a very upscale suburb of Seattle. The classes were in basic Judaism – pretty simplistic. As I looked around the classroom that first evening, what I quickly realized was that I was the only single man there. The other students were either couples or solitary women. All were there, I learned in our introductions, because they were interested in or studying for conversion. One or the other of the couples had agreed to convert for an upcoming or new marriage. And the women who were there by themselves had married Jewish guys and were trying to figure out what hoops they had to jump through to become Jewish. When it came my time to introduce myself and explain why I was there, I said, "I was born Jewish and come from a Jewish family, but I don't truly know what it means to be Jewish."

The Rabbi who would be our teacher asked, "Could you be more specific? What is it you want to learn?" He seemed perplexed, concerned that I might have stumbled into the wrong classroom.

"I don't really know that," I said. I saw that everyone was staring at me now, puzzled like the Rabbi. "I guess I just want to feel what you feel. I want to be part of something bigger than myself. I want to know who I am."

The Rabbi chuckled. "Maybe you should be going to a psychologist." Most of the rest of the group laughed along with him, though not all. I saw some of the gentile women nod in, what I imagined, was sympathy or empathy. It's probably why they were there too. The others just wanted to get their Jew license.

"I'm doing that too," I said, and sat down. As you might guess, I didn't get too far with that initial foray into Jewish life. I did go to a Friday night service at the Mercer Island Synagogue, and was not surprised to find many of the unpleasant reinforcing negative stereotypes. The women dressed to the gills and flashing heavy jewelry. The men, comfortable burghers, reeking of money and cigars, a clear hierarchy in place. I sat way in the rear. The service didn't speak to my needs. And the Rabbi never even said hello, though I knew he recognized me. I felt out of place by a mile, and ready once again to run screaming from the Jews.

Two years later I returned to Portland and a good teaching job at another Catholic high school and thought again about pursuing a reconnection with Judaism. Teaching in a Catholic school did, strangely enough, push me more toward that identification. I didn't hesitate to claim my Jewishness. In fact, on occasion, I would be asked to address a religion class about Judaism and so had to do some much needed studying to make a coherent presentation. It felt good, both the studying and the claiming of that part of who

I was. I felt the first stirrings of real pride about being a Jew. And was duly impressed by the amount of respect I received there for who I was. Maybe it took a religious environment, even if not a Jewish one, to lead me towards an appreciation of my own religion. To say, out loud, this is who I am.

All of which is not to say that I still did not have my doubts, my skepticism, not only about Judaism, but about any religion at all. Frankly, I still found it difficult to accept the idea of a supreme, all-knowing, all-controlling God. And though studying the ways in which Jewish scholars are able to explore and interpret biblical law and Torah stories, gave me new appreciation for religious scholarship and for the ways in which that could be applied in the real world, I still wondered why I had such a hard time sitting through Shabbat services, and why I didn't feel as moved by the prayers and rituals as others apparently and visibly did. Maybe I would never be able to call myself a religious Jew. Maybe my connection was simply one of culture and politics and a sense of personal identity. Which is a lot. Maybe even enough.

I keep looking. Keep going to services, talking to our Rabbi, who has become a good friend. I've been called up to the Torah for an Aliyah on Yom Kippur, given a drash during the high holy days about Jonah. I teach a class in memoir writing from a Jewish perspective at the Reconstructionist synagogue we belong to. And my wife and I went on a trip to Israel with some of our congregation.

Yes, I said my wife. I did eventually find that special soulful, dark-haired Jewish woman. Beverly and I met late in life, in our fifties. Bev had never been married before, having devoted much of her adult life to a career in progressive politics. She had even run for governor of the state shortly before we met. I was, of course, impressed by her accomplishments, but even more impressed by her optimism and generosity of spirit. Like me, she had at times sought answers about her spiritual life. She even belonged to a synagogue and was not shy about claiming her heritage. At this point in my life, I knew that if I were to have a long-term relationship with a woman, she would have to be Jewish. Bev was the one who was truly my *bashert*. The woman I will spend the rest of my life with. We had a Jewish wedding under the chuppah, sealed with a proper Ketubah we wrote ourselves. We committed to not only a life together, but also a Jewish one. I wish my mother had been there to see it. She finally would have been pleased.

Hep, Hep C

I was diagnosed with Hepatitis C virus in 1992, but I'm guessing I had been infected with it since around 1972, which is the time when I was using heroin and such, injecting the crap into my bloodstream, with whatever needles were available. Nobody knew about the virus then or that you could get infections from sharing needles with your "friends." I don't blame anyone but myself. No one forced me to behave like an idiot.

Hepatitis C, in and of itself, is not life threatening, but the virus eats away at the liver, and if left untreated will result in liver cancer, and, by all reports, that's a nasty way to go. Up until recently, there have not been very effective treatments. The first time I tried a cure I only lasted a few weeks. I was simply too debilitated by the interferon that I self-injected every day. And I had to keep working then, a single dad with a full-time teaching gig and lots of responsibilities. I couldn't function behind the meds, though the doctors had barely warned me of the nature of these "side effects" and how they would impact me.

I didn't think about it again for a number of years, ten to be exact, when a doctor at Kaiser noticed my elevated liver counts in a routine blood screening and referred me to a gastroenterologist who was specializing in treating Hep C, which was now much more well-known and recognized, as more and more of us baby boomers, former drug rats, discovered that we too were infected, even though we'd been living exemplary lives for the last 30 years. This bug does not let go easily – or at all. But the GI doc convinced me to enter into treatment once again, assuring me that the drug protocol was now much more effective and the side effects more manageable. Neither of these claims turned out to be true.

It was an eight-month process that included weekly interferon injections (a newer brew) and a daily regimen of anti-viral pills that caused me to lose a third of my body-weight. And I'm a big guy. I won't go into all the details of that harrowing time period, it would only sound self-pitying, even to me. As an example of my state of mind, though – one day, as I went on my slow, unsteady walk to the corner store – not because I needed anything, but because I had to get out of the house, if only for a few minutes – I saw a young guy, maybe a college student, riding his bike down Thurman Street, not a care in the world, I thought, and before I knew it or why, I was on my knees weeping.

Since Beverly was able to work and support me, I had the ability to devote eight months of my life to this chemotherapy extended hell – something most people would not have the luxury to do. Nor would those without good medical insurance have the financial wherewithal to undergo such an expensive therapy.

And – in the end, for me, it was not effective. "Did not clear virus" was the final entry on my chart. It felt like a death sentence. The Hep C doc gave me figures that implied I would probably not live 5 more years. In 2015 I was still kicking around. From what I could tell, the worst part of having Hepatitis C were the treatments. But, like my daughter told me, "You don't even know all the ways your health has been impacted by this." I don't just have Hep C; I have cirrhosis of the liver, caused by the virus. And it has affected the quality of my life. Lots of little aches and pains, fevers and colds, stomach distress, lack of energy. I know, that's what's called aging. But this feels like more, mainly because there's never any other reason for my various illnesses. It's all about the liver –the largest internal organ in the body, responsible for filtering all sorts of impurities out of the engine. I picture mine all scarred up, like a boxer's face. Like a piece of meat you'd never buy in a store.

After the long losing battle in 2004, I swore I was done with treatments. It wasn't worth it. But then I started hearing about a new Hep C drug that had been developed and recently approved – and, if the TV ads could be believed, it was a miracle drug. One pill a day for a couple months and the virus would up and flee the scene. I didn't trust it. I'd been lied to before. Nothing comes easy – or for free. Looked it up on line, though. And the reports seemed legit. But the story that caught my attention the most about the new drug – or drugs (there are a couple competing brands) was the obscene cost. This is not a drug for anyone who doesn't have really good insurance or is independently wealthy. A single pill costs $1,000. For a four-month regimen, the cost is $120,000. Plus the cost of the other pills that some (most?) sufferers have to take along with the super-pill. The articles I read also said, that, the entire cost of production of one of these pills, including research, would come to approximately $8 per pill – in a just world – or another more enlightened country. The drug companies were getting way fat on this one. Made me almost ready to say I'd have nothing to do with it. Almost. Funny how your principles can get pushed aside in a pinch.

So I decided to do the new treatment, which *was* easier, but not nearly as easy as the commercials would have you believe. I had to take a few other medications along with the new miracle drug, and the side effects were still difficult. Some days I didn't move from my chair. (Why do they insist on calling them side effects, when they are not off to the side at all.) But I only had to do the drugs for four months this time, and I gritted my teeth and got through it. The blood tests came back three months later (you have to wait that long to make sure the reading is accurate) and I was finally clear. The Hep C virus was gone. Hallelujah! Bev was as relieved about the news as I was. Now we could go ahead and make plans for our retirement years without the sword of Damocles hanging over our heads. And, to be fair, I have to give credit to Western medicine on this one and to the good doctor at Kaiser who shepherded me through it all.

Still it would be good if big pharma were not always looking to gouge the most money possible from the sickest among us. It's a national tragedy. What kind of society decides that quality health care is only for the rich? The bloodsuckers always seem to get fat. I was lucky, not everyone is.

Barking Dogs

Bev and I have a late-life marriage, the second for me, Bev's first after a long political career. It was hard to figure out where we wanted to live. We both owned homes, but neither seemed entirely suitable for our new coupledom. I sold my place, a sweet little one bedroom, one bath in a Portland neighborhood that had been perfect for my long singleness. I moved into Bev's condo, which had more room, but little personality. We agreed it was temporary. Eventually we'd sell it and use the proceeds from both our house sales to buy something together.

Everything we looked at seemed overpriced, especially in the inner Southeast area where we thought we wanted to live. So, to get more bang for our housing buck, we looked further north in a neighborhood our agent assured us was "up and coming." We eventually found a newish foursquare on a corner lot that we liked. It had good light, a wrap-around front porch and a fig tree in the back yard.

My only hesitancy about the new place was a concern about noise in the neighborhood. I wanted quiet, wanted it desperately. Our tenancy at the condo had ended with a screaming confrontation with a neighbor lady who left her yapping dachshund out in the yard all night long, and seemed puzzled that anyone might be offended by the ceaseless, piercing barking. Another neighbor told me she dealt with the noise by lighting a candle and trying to meditate. "How'd that work for you?" I asked.

Before we signed papers on the new house, we went and knocked on doors of all the nearby neighbors, and politely asked if there was any problem in the neighborhood with barking dogs. No, they all assured us, seemingly surprised by such a question. It was a quiet neighborhood, they all said, no problem. None of them seemed particularly friendly, except for the old lady across the street and she was hard of hearing.

The day after we moved in, the dogs began howling. Dogs – plural. From almost every direction. The Doberman right next door who went berserk anytime anybody passed by his front door, the border collie yapping incessantly behind the fenced yard, two threatening Rottweilers, who seemed to have free rein to run up and down 73rd Street. What those neighbors hadn't told us was that they were all dog owners themselves. And dog owners are apparently immune to dog noise. It's like an inoculation you get when you buy a canine, an anti-virus that affects your hearing.

I decided to take matters into my own hands. I knocked on doors, confronted neighbors, left form letters provided by Multnomah County Animal Services that threatened legal recourses. Nothing worked. The dogs kept howling and I became more and more sensitized to the noise. The slightest yip would set me off: my stomach churned, my heart raced, and I became instantly and unreasonably angry. I didn't know how to let it go. Once that barking started, I was fully engaged and no amount of self-talk or deep breathing could help. In the truest sense, I was becoming a madman. And the neighbors were on to me.

One of them came knocking on our front door, an older guy, 80ish, wearing a baseball cap and overalls, smiling crookedly. Without preliminaries, he asked, "What's the matter with you people? Don't you like dogs?"

"What?" I said. "Who the hell are you?"

"I live up the street." He flung an arm out toward the right. "I'll say it again. Don't you people like dogs?"

I gave him a hard stare. "I like some dogs," I said. "It depends."

"On what?"

"On their owners," I said.

Bev had come downstairs by then, alerted by the loud voices, and stood beside me.

"The other neighbors don't much care for all your complaining," he continued. "We think you must not like dogs."

All thoughts of maintaining neighborly relations drained away. "Dogs are like people," I said. "If you don't teach them good manners, they're a real pain in the ass."

The old guy's jaw dropped. Clearly he hadn't anticipated opposition. I was ready to slam the door in his face as final punctuation, but Bev put a gentling hand on my shoulder and stepped in front of me. "Hi," she said, "thanks for stopping by. Would you like to come inside so we can discuss this? I'm sure we both have our concerns."

I started to protest, but caught my breath and stepped to the side. The neighbor guy too seemed to calm down, even took his cap into his hand, smiled at Beverly, and shuffled inside. Five minutes later he was playing his harmonica for us. Don't ask me why. Bev and he exchanged phone numbers and each promised to call if there were any further problems.

Still, the dogs continued to bark. I took to sleeping with earplugs, and playing the radio loudly during the day. But in the end, after two years, we gave in and put the house up for sale and started looking once again.

After a couple more futile attempts to find quiet and peace of mind in the city, Bev and I moved out of Portland to a small town on the Coast. It's quiet here and we are (finally) happy with our home and neighborhood. I feel more settled, more able to deal with distractions when they come along. I've even rekindled my love of dogs, happy to see them frolicking on the beach – might some day get one of my own. And we know our neighbors – almost all of them. I'm sure if there were ever a problem, we could talk to them about it without hard feelings. Maybe it's just the pace of life that eases the strain. City life – for me had become too stressful. I think that must be true for many people.

Writing While You Wait

I knew I was being played. It was the journals they were after. The aim was to score a free notebook, not to be in a writing group. What I didn't realize was how much value these blank books had in the prison setting, a place where personal possessions were limited, if not altogether absent.

"Hey, man, could I get one for my girlfriend? It would mean a lot to her."

The other inmates looked at me, waiting for my response, waiting to see how soft I might be.

"No, sorry," I said. "I'm only allotted one journal for each participant."

"Looks like there's more than that," a guy across the table sneered. I looked over at him, a thin, pockmarked man, with a tattoo of some sort showing above his collar. He'd printed "Lenny" on the name card that sat in front of him.

I met his stare. "There might be extra now," I said, at the same time gathering together the remaining journals on the table top and slipping them into my briefcase, "But we could get other writers in later. Or maybe someone will lose theirs and need a replacement."

Of course, the next week, lost journals were endemic.

So began the writing workshop that I was facilitating at a local jail, situated on the outskirts of North Portland. I was working with a volunteer organization that conducts ten week long creative writing workshops across a broad spectrum of disadvantaged and distressed populations. For the most part, these are folks who normally would not have access to group workshops, and often people who have little experience with writing of any sort. The results are often spectacular, and for a facilitator the discoveries are a joy to watch.

I had previously done workshops in homeless shelters, and residential housing facilities, and one for a senior LGBT group. Prison was different, though. Nobody fought over journals in my gay old-folks group, and I didn't have to count the number of pens returned to me in my workshop at the Old Town housing facility. No one there was likely to sneak one out to use as a shank. And I didn't have to go through a metal detector or empty out my pockets before entering those facilities.

On the other hand, I had found in my previous session at the jail, that once all the distractions and games were moved to the side, these guys proved to be some of the most serious and talented writers I had dealt with anywhere, including my ten years of college teaching. There was an almost palpable need I could feel in that locked, gray, classroom. And once the group learned to trust me and each other, and trust that they weren't being manipulated, they looked forward to our sessions with unusual enthusiasm. "You know, this is the best two hours of my week," one guy confessed to me. Admittedly, I didn't have much competition. Aside from the two hours of creative stretching we did in class, the inmates spent their other 166 hours under constant observation and regimentation and without a moment of privacy or quiet. I had visited the dorms a couple of times, and had to try very hard to cover my feelings of horror and fear. I don't think those two words are hyperbole. I know I couldn't breathe by the time I got out of there, even though I was impressed by the seeming friendliness and openness of the men. "You make the best of your situation, you learn to go with it," an old-timer told me. Still, the major thing I learned about jail from the time I spent there, was that I would never ever, no matter what, allow myself to be incarcerated. One of the things that most disturbed me about their living conditions was that the men had almost no access to the outside. There was one exercise room, which was technically outdoors – you could look up and see the sky (usually cloudy in Portland), but the walls were without windows and rose ten feet tall, so that no view was possible. Seasons were largely indistinguishable from that tiny patch of cement gray sky.

From the moment you entered this (so-called) correctional facility, till the time you picked up your car keys and personal belongings from the front desk officer and signed out, there was no sense that any world existed outside of that grim place. I think I represented a danger in that regard. I had the potential to bring the outside world in, if only in the form of stories and ideas. I felt as if I was viewed with suspicion by the guards and the deputies. *Another stupid ass do-gooder,* is probably what they thought. *Doesn't know who he's dealing with.* When the head guard led me to the classroom I would use, he pointed out the red emergency button on the wall. "Only push that if you're really in a jam," he said. Then he added, "Of course, by the time we get here, it might be too late." I couldn't tell if this was a joke.

Jail is a hard place. Life distilled down to its bleakest measures. I never met an inmate who didn't seem to be unconsciously looking over his shoulder. It's a dangerous, paranoid environment, with only the slightest, minimal bow to humanity and decency. And maybe that's the way it's supposed to be. I didn't kid myself that the guys I was working with were there for a reason. They had done bad things, hurt people, sometimes killed them. Although for my own sense of sanity and fairness, I decided I didn't want to know what their individual crimes were. I suspected that knowing a guy was an alleged murderer or a rapist or someone who beat the shit out of his wife might color my perception of him. The only way I wanted to know these men was through their writing. I wasn't there to be their friend or their judge. We were all there only as writers. What I asked them to write, I wrote myself. If the prompt was, "What people should know about me" I attacked it with the same enthusiasm and honesty as I expected they would.

I told these men, "I don't care about you." I paused and took in their stares, the incipient movement toward anger. "I only care about your stories." I'd let that sink in for a minute or two, watch the heads nod in recognition. *Yeah, man, I get it. This cat is interested in my work; he's treating me like a person.* Usually, I couldn't help adding, after a minute or two, "Well, I do actually care about you." There would be laughter, a release. Then we could go ahead and write.

"Always come back to the writing. That's why we're there," my support person told me. It was worth remembering. Especially in a group that at times had a tendency to want to complain or gossip. Even in their stories, there was a tendency toward heavy drama, self-aggrandizing, soap opera riffs. Or with some guys, a focus on easy spirituality – as in, now that I've discovered Jesus, everything is fixed. Sometimes there's not a lot a facilitator can do with that type of writing except try to gently push them in a more authentic direction. I found that the best technique for getting writers to get real was to let the rest of the group have at them. Though always in a positive way. That was one of the guidelines we established for feedback right off the dime. All comments had to be positive. This could be perplexing. "How'm I gonna tell him what's wrong with his story if I can't say anything bad about it?" someone would invariably ask.

"Think of it as an observation. Not a judgment." I said. "Tell him what you think. Just don't tear the story down. You wouldn't like it if someone did that to you."

When we'd go over this, then put it into practice, the writers would see that you could say just about anything you wanted to as long as it was done in a gentle and supportive way. I thought more than a few times that many of the college writing classes and critique groups I'd been involved with over the years would have benefitted from this rule. All the picky, intellectualized criticism in those seminars did little except upset the participants and leave a bitter aftertaste about the whole business of writing.

One of my favorite prompts to begin a class with is the simple two-word phrase, "I remember. . ." I tell them to keep their pens moving, to forget about all those things they may have been taught about "proper writing," to allow themselves the freedom to mess up, to write crap, or to lose track of reason. "If you get stuck," I say, "go ahead and write nonsense or copy out your name twenty times, pretty soon you'll come back to where you want to be." It's rare, extremely so, that participants don't find words, lots of them, to fill up the pages of their journals. Some do actually need a fresh journal by the time we're near the end of the session. And many new writers report back that "not a day goes by now that I don't write in my journal."

I don't know what the inmates did when I was no longer there to provide a journal and a pen. The only writing utensils they were allowed were golf-score pencils, those damn little stubs you can barely get a grip on. The guards didn't allow any objects that could be used as weapons. But the men managed to use what they had. James, a pink cheeked young man, told me that he'd seen someone use the golf pencil to put another inmate's eye out. "He stuck the pencil between his fingers like this," James said, pressing the little yellow stub between the fingers of his clenched fist so that the point just jutted out. "Then he punched the dude in the head."

"Man, I don't want to hear that," I said.

"I didn't say nothing," James responded with a grin.

A week later, on coming into the classroom, James reached down into his grayish sock and pulled out a piece of hard candy, which he flipped over to me. All the rest of the men stared, with what looked like longing. "Thanks," I said, and shoved the linty candy into my pocket. I didn't get till later that a piece of candy was an important gift, as rare a treat as a visit from an old girlfriend. I should have shown more appreciation. (Although according to the rules, I should have not accepted the candy at all.) There was a lot I still needed to learn.

There wasn't a lot of prison bravado in our workshop sessions. And it was rare that a participant would write about his crime or the life that led him to it. They were happier with poetry and short fiction. Like all of us, they preferred escape to reality. After all, reality was smacking them across the jaw almost every other hour of the day. Much better to retreat to the solace and safety of a poem about rain, about the remembered trip to the Oregon Coast, about a baby daughter.

You were young and innocent
Gone before I knew it
If only I could
Build something with you
You were too little
To say good-bye

My heart still aches in sadness
No one will ever know
What it meant to lose you

Randy W.

Sure there was the occasional prison philosopher, the guy who wouldn't let anyone else forget where they were and how (he thought) that world operated. He was the hard-edged guy with his book of con wisdom, cynicism as higher knowledge, hate masquerading as self-protection. Lenny filled that role in this workshop session. He was hard core in every sense of the word. Lenny let the group know early and often that he'd spent 27 of his forty-four years in the slammer. His attitude, his affect, the way he tensed his shoulders, the way he stared at me, all spoke the message: Nobody can break me, no matter what, cause I'm smarter and meaner than any of you bastards. At the end of our second class, when I was about to buzz the guard to come and collect the men, he sidled up to me and handed me one of the ballpoint pens I handed out at the beginning of the class, and, neglectfully, had failed to collect from him. Lenny grinned as he handed it to me, *See, man,* he was saying without saying it, *I can go right around you anytime I want.* I'd been told a hundred times to make sure I left with all the same things I came in with. "You can take those apart and use them to shoot up," Lenny muttered. "At least that's what I've been told." I was embarrassed and a little pissed off, but still there was something about this man I admired, even as I feared him. It was probably the same response he got from the other inmates, a grudging, but careful, respect.

At first, I couldn't quite figure out why he wanted to be in the writing group. What was his game here? My first guess was that it was simply to ameliorate the boredom of incarceration and to have a soapbox for his posturing and platitudes. When given room, Lenny would go on for long stretches at a time, weaving his diatribe, his language as coarse as you might expect. I would step in and stop him when he got going, but made sure to do it as non-confrontationally as I could. Surprisingly, he didn't get angry when I told him it was time to let others speak or read or even when I asked him to respect the situation by not cursing. Another long-timer later explained to me, that, "Lenny's top dog in the dorm, but in here you're the alpha man." As incapable of doing anyone injury as I was, in this environment, any real authority was on my side. I wasn't an inmate.

As the weeks went by, I started to see that the reason Lenny was in the writing group was not about getting over on anybody or avoiding work duty. He was there because he really wanted to write. As hard as his life had been and as tough as he was, underneath all the bullshit, what he truly wanted was to be heard. Lenny, just like all the other men, saw that writing was a way to escape the external situation he was in and find a place within himself more worthwhile, something that hadn't been beaten out of him. Writing gave Lenny hope. It gave him a shot at a different reality.

If I could go back,
I'd change the time

That I haven't spent
With you,
I'd change all the hurt
and pain
I put you through,
I'd change the fact
That I miss you.
Because I'd change
Everyday that I'm
Away from you.

Lenny R

We ended our ten-week workshop with a reading. Of course, it couldn't be a public reading, but the guys would be allowed to invite one guest each from the rest of the prison population. My one ally at the jail, Jayne, a counselor, had helped me to arrange the program, and, miraculously, had even managed to get donuts and sodas for the night of the reading, an unheard of treat. My support person from the agency also came, and brought a nicely typeset program that listed the names of all the readers and the names of their poems and stories. I handed one to each participant as they filed in and watched as they slowly took in what they were holding and what it represented to them. Their shoulders squared, their eyes bright as they sat and inhaled their names off the page. With eleven readers and eleven guests, the room felt crowded, and formal, in a very positive way. We managed to forget about the closed-circuit TV cameras that were always watching. This was our event and as each man rose to read and was greeted by a respectful silence and enthusiastic applause when he finished, the sense of accomplishment continued to rise. In a room full mostly of hardened men, I thought I noticed more than a few wet cheeks. And when the last reader was done and Jayne announced that it was time for refreshments, the men politely, even delicately, helped themselves to a donut and paper cup of soda. Nobody pushed or tried to take more than one. A box of donuts in the dorm would probably occasion a riot. It was as if everyone (writers and guests both) knew that this kind of night, this kind of experience required a different and better sort of behavior than what was normally expected and given. It proved to me yet again, the power that writing has – both in the composing and the hearing – to transform lives, or to allow one to rise above his circumstances. In here, in the depths of this damn jail, we had done that.

The Next Wave

I wake up early so I can hit the beach at high tide. It's the middle of January on the Oregon Coast, rainy and cold, but I don't care. I'm happy as I tug on my wetsuit. Twenty minutes later I'm out in the Pacific Ocean, jumping over the incoming waves on my body-board. The light rain has turned to sleet, but I don't feel cold. I look back at the beach and the jetties, then out toward where the bigger waves are breaking, and I paddle out that way.

I had surfed when I was a kid, back in New Jersey. Yes, there's surfing in New Jersey, even if the waves are not particularly gnarly. I loved being in the ocean. My family spent summers on Long Beach Island for as long as I could remember. Eventually we bought a little cottage. I think my father had dreams of retiring there, but he died before that could happen. I always thought summer was the best time of the year; it was my release from the dreariness of Philadelphia and what I considered, my gray life. Summer was bright and yellow; it was when I was alive, when I was full of juice, when I was in the ocean for hours every day.

At first, it was body surfing, which is a pretty exciting thing to do, if you know how to do it right. I was a good body surfer, knew just when to dive ahead of the wave to catch the best ride. It was always thrilling to go rocketing into shore at what felt like a hundred miles an hour. You have to hold your position to get the best and longest ride, hands pointed out in front, body solid, and not lose your position even when the wave crashes onto the beach. If you're riding it right, your body slides smoothly on to the wet sand, without even a scratch, but if you lose your form, or try to bail, the wave will crack you down onto the beach, twisted and bruised. But what the hell, getting hurt was not a big deal. When I wiped out, I'd pick myself up and run back into the surf, looking for the next big wave. I could, and often did, body surf all day long.

Surfboards didn't come around till the early sixties (at least in New Jersey), and I wasn't on board right away, because there was an investment to be made and a surfboard didn't come cheaply. Mom and Dad did not approve of me wasting my money from summer jobs, money that I was supposed to be saving for college. I could have told them that I'd rather be a surfer than a college student, but that was not the kind of statement that would have proved beneficial to my health or well being. If you were a Jewish boy, you went to college. Especially if your father was a doctor and had big hopes for you. Still I managed to do some surfing on borrowed boards, but not enough to get really good at it, and at the end of the summer of 1962, I went off to college in Ohio, nowhere near an ocean, and didn't much think of becoming a surfer again. I mean, that's the way it is. You're either gonna follow the waves, or follow the rules.

I never did fulfill my family wishes for me. Was not a diligent college student. Probably missed more classes than I attended, and was in no way qualified to apply for medical school when I graduated, which was when my father pretty much gave up on me. Or maybe that happened earlier, when I told them I was going to change my major to English. "And do what?" Dad asked.

"I don't know," I mumbled, "Teach maybe? Write?"

Dad snorted and held his newspaper up in front of his face, which is what he always did when he was through with a conversation. After that, I hardly even went down the Shore anymore. Forgot about surfing. Eventually moved away to the West Coast, to Seattle. I still loved the ocean, though the waters in Puget Sound and off the Washington Coast were always frigid, even in the summer time. All you could do was hold your breath and plunge in, then rush out before you developed hypothermia. Even body surfing was out of the question; the waves were just too unpredictable, the beach too rocky. And, anyway, I was raising a family by then, holding down a teaching job, struggling with an unhappy marriage. Being an adult. Feeling way older than my years.

Many years passed. Many. Damn it all. And somehow, I never did get back to surfing. Even though we were now living in Oregon and the Oregon Coast had a thriving surfer community, but I was playing it safe. Or maybe that's just another way to say I was scared. But scared of what? It wasn't the ocean or the waves I feared, or even the cold. I knew about wet suits, and I wanted to go, would spend hours at a time some days watching the surfers out on the waves in Seaside. Maybe I was scared I wouldn't be able to cut it anymore, that I would look foolish and fall. Or that the real surfers would think I was too old to be on a board. Or maybe I was scared that my knees were too creaky now to get up.

Yeah, all those things were going on, but what was really holding me back was the unshakeable, though deeply submerged, feeling that I didn't deserve to enjoy myself. That surfing was self-indulgent, and that at my age (40ish!) I had to be serious, dignified. You never would have caught my father out surfing. Even after Dad passed away I still felt his eyes and his judgement on me. I still needed to please him. And how about this for a reason I didn't go surfing all those years? I was a dumbass. And I can't blame that on anybody but myself.

But even dumbasses sometimes get a chance at redemption. On my 70th birthday, I rented a wetsuit and a long board and went surfing. For the first time in 50 years. And I loved it. All the old excitement was there, the adrenalin coursed through my veins, the best drug in the world. Of course, I fell that day way more than I got up, and probably the other surfers looked at me with a mixture of amusement and disdain, but I didn't ever think about it; I was way too busy for that. It was only after I became so exhausted that I could no longer make another attempt and reluctantly paddled back to shore to my waiting wife and grown daughter, who were cheering me on, that I was able to think about what had just happened in my life.

Yes, I'd spent a few hours in the ocean, felt pleasantly worn out, and pleased with myself; but there was something more going on. Something had shifted. I knew right away that I would keep on surfing now – one way or another – but also that I had finally reached a place where it was okay to do the kind of things I wanted to do. Age and seriousness of purpose were no longer acceptable excuses.

Over the next few months, I came to realize that for me, surfing could be an integral part of my life, and a metaphor that might keep me going for longer than I would have otherwise. I now live at the Coast, and the first thing I do each morning is go out on our deck and check the waves. If the surf looks promising, I quickly get on my wetsuit and go. Often Beverly comes with me. She worries about me, I know, but she still smiles and tells me to have a good time as she goes for a long walk on the beach while I play. She and I both know that what I'm doing is not safe. There are rip tides that could quickly pull me far away from shore. Most days there is no one around who I could even wave to. And I've wiped out plenty, sometimes slammed down so hard that I come up without any idea where the shoreline is and hoping my board won't come back and smack me in the head. The other day a surfer was attacked by a shark not far from my favorite spot. Still I tell Bev not to worry. If I'm going to go, this is how I want to do it.

Surfing (or since my knees exploded, bodyboarding)

has become for me a touchstone for my later years. Being in the ocean, riding a hard breaking wave, is my reminder to let go, relax. There is nothing but right now, right here. Present tense, baby. Once again, I am a happy beach bum.

Acknowledgements

Some of the pieces included in this book have appeared previously in the following publications: Purple Clover, Jewish Literary Journal, North Coast Squid, Philadelphia Stories, Under The Gum Tree, and Thereby Hangs a Tale.

I want to thank all the people who helped me put this collection together – primarily my wife, partner, and surfing Sherpa – Beverly Stein. Bev also took the photo for the front cover. My two lovely daughters, Jessica and Gabrielle Freedman, I thank for putting up with my ongoing invasion of their privacy. I hope they're used to it by now. Thanks also to Catherine Rolling, who has been a better sport about my public (and one-sided) explorations of our early family life than I ever would have been.

I've been lucky to have worked with a number of excellent writers and teachers over the years. Most prominently: Ana Ramana, Ariel Gore, and Rebecca Brown. All women. Hmmm.

And thanks to the writers who have influenced my work – too many to mention, though Raymond Carver, J.D. Salinger, and Alice Munro must be. It's also been my great fortune and pleasure to facilitate writing groups over the last ten years at Write Around Portland, the Multnomah Arts Center, and at Havurah Shalom. Thanks must go also to all the brilliant students I've worked with. I've learned so much from them.

Much love also to my sister and brother, Linda and Paul Freedman, whose recollections of events may, in some cases differ widely from my own. Such is the nature of memoir.

About the Author

Robert "Butch" Freedman

A long-time writer and teacher, Butch lives in Cape Meares, Oregon, with his wife, Beverly Stein. Originally from Philadelphia, he has finally fully acclimated to life in the Great Northwest. He still roots for the Phillies, though.

Butch published the autobiographical novel Fancypants—A Bar Mitzvah Tale in 2008. His short prose works have appeared in numerous publications, including: *Purple Clover, Drash, Tikkun, Philadelphia Stories, Still Crazy, Under the Gum Tree, Northwest Squid,* and *Portland Magazine.* One of his short stories was nominated for a Pushcart Prize.

He has facilitated writing workshops for Write Around Portland (some at Inverness Jail), at Havurah Shalom, and at the Multnomah Arts Center.

CPSIA information can be obtained
at www.ICGtesting.com
Printed in the USA
BVHW07s1130091018
529682BV00003B/305/P

9 781629 015682